TOPICS IN MATHEMATICS

TRANSLATED FROM THE RUSSIAN

ALGORITHMS AND AUTOMATIC COMPUTING MACHINES

B. A. TRAKHTENBROT

D. C. HEATH AND COMPANY

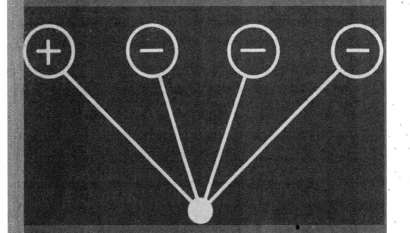

TOPICS IN MATHEMATICS

Algorithms and Automatic Computing Machines

B. A. Trakhtenbrot

Translated and adapted from the second Russian edition (1960) by

JEROME KRISTIAN, JAMES D. McCAWLEY, *and* SAMUEL A. SCHMITT

SURVEY OF

RECENT EAST EUROPEAN MATHEMATICAL LITERATURE

A project conducted by

ALFRED L. PUTNAM *and* IZAAK WIRSZUP

*Department of Mathematics,
The University of Chicago, under a
grant from the National Science Foundation*

D. C. HEATH AND COMPANY   BOSTON

PREFACE TO THE AMERICAN EDITION

ALTHOUGH ALGORITHMS have been known and used since antiquity, the theory of algorithms has been developed almost entirely in the twentieth century. Fundamental to the theory is the question of algorithmic solvability and unsolvability. In defining rigorously the term *algorithm* the author considers the close relation between algorithms and computing machines. Indeed, he proves the algorithmic unsolvability of several problems using a special type of computing machine called the *Turing machine*.

The reader will need no specific information from other branches of mathematics beyond intermediate algebra to be able to read the book. However, he will have to be able to follow a rather complex train of logical thought.

References to several of the topics discussed are given in the Bibliography.

CONTENTS

Algorithms and Automatic Computing Machines

Introduction

Since 1948 there has been great progress in the development of automatic high-speed computing machines, which are now used to solve many kinds of mathematical and logical problems. The feature which distinguishes these machines from earlier calculating machines is automatic control. Once the initial data and the program are fed into a machine and the machine is set running, it works through to the final answer without any human intervention. The productivity of modern electronic machines is enormous. They can carry out as many as 20,000 arithmetic operations in one second,[1] which is far more than a skilled operator could do in a whole day's work on a good calculating machine.

The range of application of automatic machines keeps growing: machines solve complicated systems of equations, translate from one language to another, play chess, etc. They are used in large factories to control technological processes. Also, the fact that experimental data can be analyzed rapidly and accurately by machines makes possible the use of hitherto impractical methods of research in many scientific fields. In general, automatic computing machines are already recognized as powerful tools for freeing people completely from certain types of laborious tasks.

But these real accomplishments have given rise to many unfounded illusions and fantastic predictions about all-powerful machines. In particular, we might mention stories of "giant electronic brains," and of automata which can solve any problem and thus replace creative research. In view of this, the question of what actually *can* be done by computing machines becomes very important and timely. This question is answered from one point of view in the modern theory of algorithms, an important branch of mathematical logic.

Mathematical logic investigates the nature of such concepts as "calculation process," "mathematical proof," and "algorithm." Several years before the invention of modern electronic machines, an exact definition of "algorithm" and a general scheme for an automatic computing machine (the Turing machine, Chapter 8,

---

[1] This number is constantly increasing.

described in 1936 in a paper [1][1] on the theory of algorithms) were worked out, and the close connection between algorithms and machines was clarified. This formed the basis for a series of important theorems about automatic machines; in particular, it was proved rigorously that there are problems which machines cannot solve. We shall discuss some of these matters in this book.

In sections 1–4 we explain what an algorithm is and construct algorithms for the solution of certain classes of mathematical and logical problems.

In sections 5–6 we discuss the principles of organization of electronic computing machines, as well as *programming* (the construction of algorithms designed to be executed by machines).

In sections 7–13 we present a number of important facts from the theory of algorithms, based on the concept of the Turing machine.

The length of many proofs makes it impossible to include them in a book of this size, but this lack of complete detail should make it easier to grasp the general outline of the subject.

Modern automatic machines are called *electronic* because the main element in their construction is the electron tube (and more recently the transistor). The use of electronic techniques provides a great saving of time in the individual operations performed by a machine. However, the basic feature of these machines—automatic control—is independent of the use of electronics. In principle, one could build a mechanical automatic computing machine which would solve the same problems as the electronic machines (although it would be much slower); we cannot consider the development of modern computing machines to be solely the result of progress in electronics. In fact, the first general scheme[2] for an automatic computing machine (the Turing machine) was in terms of a mechanical system. The first machine actually constructed (1940) was electro-mechanical.

We shall not go into the technical details of machine construction but shall discuss chiefly the function and interaction of the various parts of computers, confining ourselves to their mathematical and logical aspects.

[1] See Bibliography on page 101.

[2] Translators' Note: The author is apparently unaware of the *Analytical Engine* of Charles Babbage, originally conceived in the 1830's, although never built. Babbage envisioned a mechanical device consisting of a 1000-word memory, an arithmetic unit, a control unit, and input-output devices. It involved the program's being stored as a stack of punched cards (!).

1. Numerical Algorithms

The concept of algorithm is one of the basic concepts of mathematics. By an *algorithm* is meant a list of instructions specifying a sequence of operations which will give the answer to any problem of a given type. Of course, this is not a precise mathematical definition of the term, but it gives the sense of such a definition. It reflects the concept of algorithm which arose naturally and has been used in mathematics since ancient times.

The simplest algorithms are the rules for performing the four arithmetic operations on numbers written in decimal form. (The term "algorithm" comes from the name of a medieval Uzbek mathematician, al-Khowārizmī, who gave such rules as early as the ninth century.) For example, the addition of two multidigit numbers consists of a series of elementary operations, each of which involves only two digits (one of which may be a stroke to denote a one carried from the previous step). These operations are of two types: (1) writing down the sum of corresponding digits; (2) marking the carrying of a one to the left. The instructions give the proper order for performing these operations (from right to left). The elementary operations are purely formal in that they can be carried out automatically, using an addition table which can be written down once and for all without reference to any particular problem.

The situation is analogous for the other three arithmetic operations, for the extraction of square roots, etc. The formal character of the corresponding instructions (algorithms) is readily apparent, especially in the procedure for extracting square roots.

1. THE EUCLIDEAN ALGORITHM

As a further example we shall consider the *Euclidean algorithm* for solving all problems of the following type.

Given two positive integers a and b, find their greatest common divisor.

Obviously, there are as many different problems of this type as there are different pairs of positive integers a and b. Any of these problems can be solved by constructing a descending sequence of numbers, the first of which is the larger of the two given numbers, the second the smaller. The third number is the remainder from dividing the first by the second; the fourth number is the remainder from dividing the second by the third, and so on. This process is repeated until one of the divisions leaves no remainder. The divisor in this last division is then the required number.

Since division can be reduced to repeated subtraction, the algorithm for solving any such problem can be put in the form of the following list of instructions.

Instruction 1. Consider the pair of numbers a, b. Proceed to the next instruction.

Instruction 2. Compare the two numbers under consideration (that is, determine whether the first equals, is less than, or is greater than the second). Proceed to the next instruction.

Instruction 3. If the numbers are equal, then each of them is the required result; the calculation stops. If not, proceed to the next instruction.

Instruction 4. If the first number is smaller than the second, interchange them and proceed to the next instruction.

Instruction 5. Subtract the second number from the first and replace the two numbers under consideration by the subtrahend and the remainder, respectively. Proceed to instruction 2.

Thus, after carrying out all five instructions we return again to the second instruction, then the third, then the fourth, then the fifth, then back once more to the second, third, etc., until the condition given in instruction 3 is met, that is, until the two numbers under consideration are equal. When that happens the problem is solved and computation stops.

While it is true that algorithms are not always presented with such pedantic formality, there is no doubt in anyone's mind that it is possible to present any known algorithm in this formal fashion.

In the instructions for the Euclidean algorithm, the basic operations from which the process is constructed are the operations of subtracting, comparing, and interchanging two numbers. It is easy to see that these could be broken down much further; for example, instruction 5 could be expanded into a separate algorithm for subtracting one number from another. However, since the rules which govern the arithmetic operations in such cases are very simple and familiar, it is unnecessary to describe the algorithm in greater detail.

2. NUMERICAL ALGORITHMS

Algorithms based on the use of the four arithmetic operations are called *numerical algorithms*.[1] They play an important role in both elementary and advanced mathematics and are usually given in the form of verbal instructions or various kinds of formulas or schemata. For example, an algorithm for solving a system of two linear equations in two unknowns,

$$\left.\begin{aligned} a_1x + b_1y = c_1, \\ a_2x + b_2y = c_2, \end{aligned}\right\}$$

is given by the formulas

$$x = \frac{c_1b_2 - c_2b_1}{a_1b_2 - a_2b_1}, \quad y = \frac{a_1c_2 - a_2c_1}{a_1b_2 - a_2b_1},$$

in which the operations as well as their order are completely specified. The formulas give the same chain of operations for all problems of the given type (that is, for any coefficients a_1, a_2, b_1, b_2, c_1, c_2, provided $a_1b_2 - a_2b_1 \neq 0$).

It is interesting to note, however, that generally speaking the number of operations which must be performed in solving a particular problem is not known beforehand; it depends on the particular problem and is discovered only in the course of carrying out the algorithm. This is the case for the Euclidean algorithm, where the number of subtractions required depends upon the particular choice of the numbers a and b.

Numerical algorithms are widely used, since many other operations can be reduced to the four arithmetic operations. Usually such a reduction does not give an exact answer, but does give an answer to any desired accuracy. This is illustrated by the algorithm for taking a square root. By a series of divisions, multiplications, and subtractions, a root can be computed as accurately as desired. In a special branch of mathematics (*numerical analysis*) similar methods are developed for reducing to arithmetic operations more complicated operations such as integration, differentiation, and solving various kinds of equations.

In mathematics, *a class of problems is considered solved when an algorithm for solving them is found.* The discovery of such algorithms is a natural aim of mathematics. For example, algorithms have been

[1] One should keep in mind that this term has no precise meaning.

5

found for determining the number (and multiplicity) of roots of an algebraic equation and for calculating the roots to any preassigned degree of accuracy.

If there is no algorithm for solving all problems of a given type, a mathematician may be able to invent a procedure which solves certain problems of that type, although it is inapplicable to other cases.

3. DIOPHANTINE EQUATIONS

As an example of a class of problems for which present-day mathematics does not have an algorithm, let us consider all possible Diophantine equations, that is, equations of the form

$$P = 0,$$

where P is a polynomial with integral coefficients, for which integral solutions are to be sought.[1] Examples of such equations are

$$x^2 + y^2 - z^2 = 0,$$
$$6x^{18} - x + 3 = 0;$$

the first is an equation in three unknowns, and the second is an equation in one unknown. (In general, we may consider equations in any number of unknowns.) Thus, the first equation above has the integral solution

$$x = 3, \quad y = 4, \quad z = 5.$$

But the second has no integral solutions, since it is easily shown that for any integer x,

$$6x^{18} > x - 3.$$

In 1901, at an international mathematical congress in Paris, the prominent German mathematician David Hilbert presented a list of twenty unsolved problems and directed the attention of the mathematical community to the importance of solving them. Among these was the following (Hilbert's Tenth Problem): *Find an algorithm for determining whether any given Diophantine equation has an integral solution.*

---

[1] Other definitions of Diophantine equations are sometimes given.

For the particular case of Diophantine equations in one un-known, such an algorithm is known. If an equation

$$a_n x^n + a_{n-1} x^{n-1} + \cdots + a_1 x + a_0 = 0$$

with integral coefficients has an integral solution x_0, then a_0 is di-visible by x_0. This suggests the following algorithm:

(1) Find all divisors of the number a_0 (there are only a finite number of them, and there is an algorithm for finding all of them).

(2) Substitute each of these in turn into the left-hand side of the equation and calculate the resulting value.

(3) If any of the divisors gives a value of zero for the left side, then this divisor is a root of the equation; if none of the divisors gives the value zero, then the equation has no integral roots.

Hilbert's problem has been and continues to be worked on by many prominent mathematicians, but for the general case with two or more unknowns the required algorithm has not yet been found. Furthermore, it now appears very likely that such an algorithm will never be found. The exact meaning of this seemingly pessimistic prediction will be made clear to the reader later (section 44).

From the examples given so far it is apparent that numerical algorithms (and indeed, algorithms in general) possess the follow-ing characteristics:

The deterministic nature of algorithms. An algorithm must be given in the form of a finite list of instructions giving the exact pro-cedure to be followed at each step of the calculation. Thus, the cal-culation does not depend on the calculator; it is a deterministic process which can be repeated successfully at any time and by anyone.

The generality of algorithms. An algorithm is a *single* list of in-structions defining a calculation which may be carried out on *any* initial data and which in each case gives the correct result. In other words, an algorithm tells how to solve not just one particular prob-lem, but a whole class of similar problems.

2. Algorithms for Games

The examples considered in the preceding section were taken from arithmetic, algebra, and number theory. They are quite typical of the problems of those branches of mathematics and of classical mathematics in general. In this and subsequent sections we shall analyze two classes of problems which have a somewhat different character; it would be more proper to call them *logical* rather than mathematical problems, although it is hard to draw a sharp line between such *logical* problems and ordinary *mathematical* problems. But regardless of where this line is drawn or which side of it we are on, our task still remains that of finding an algorithm which gives a single method of solving any problem in some class of similar problems, the only difference being that in the cases considered here the algorithms will no longer be numerical.

4. "ELEVEN MATCHES" GAME

One of many games[1] which depend not on the outcome of chance events but on the ingenuity of the players is the game "Eleven matches."

Eleven objects, say matches, are on a table. The first player picks up 1, 2, or 3 of the matches. Then the second player picks up 1, 2, or 3 of the remaining matches. Then it is again the first player's turn to pick up 1, 2, or 3 matches. The players keep taking turns until there are no more matches. The player who is forced to pick up the last match is the *loser*. Is there any scheme by which A, the player who has the first turn, can always force his opponent B to pick up the last match?

An analysis of the game shows that A can force B to pick up the last match if he follows the following instructions:

1. *First move.* A picks up two matches.

---

[1] Translators' Note: The word "game" is used in two senses, as illustrated by the examples "Chess is a fascinating *game*" and "I played four *games* of chess today." As is customary in American writings in the theory of games, the word "game" is reserved for the first of these uses and the word "play" is used in the second sense. An individual decision made by a player during a play of a game is called a *move* of that play.

2. *Subsequent moves.* If B picks up l matches ($l \leq 3$) on his last move, then A picks up $4 - l$ matches.

It can be shown that this list of instructions is complete in the sense that regardless of what his opponent does, the list always specifies a unique move which A can make.

Such a complete list of instructions is called a *strategy* in the theory of games. If player A must necessarily win whenever he employs some strategy, it is called a *winning strategy for A*.

The strategy given for A is in fact a winning strategy, since it enables A to win regardless of what B does. This is illustrated in the following two examples:

```
A B A B A B    A B A B A B
2 2 2 1 3 1    2 3 1 1 3 1.
```

Furthermore, it can be proved that if A were to pick either one or three matches on the first move, then there would be a strategy which B could use so as to be sure of winning.

5. "EVEN WINS" GAME

Let us now consider the game "Even wins." The game starts with 27 matches on a table. The players alternately pick up from one to four of the matches. The winner is the one who has an even number of matches when all the matches have been picked up.

The following is a winning strategy for A, the player who moves first:

1. *First move.* A picks up two matches.

2. *Subsequent moves when B, the other player, has an even number of matches.* Let r be the remainder obtained upon dividing the number of matches still on the table by 6. If $r = 2$, 3, 4, or 5, then A takes (respectively) 1, 2, 3, or 4 matches.

3. *Subsequent moves when B has an odd number of matches.* If $r = 0$, 1, 2, or 3 and there are at least four matches on the table, then A takes (respectively) 1, 2, 3, or 4 matches. If $r = 4$, then A takes four matches. If there are 1 or 3 matches on the table, then A takes them all.

For example, consider the following play, in which A wins by employing this strategy:

```
A B A B A B A B A B A B
2 1 1 3 1 3.4 1 4 2 4 1.
```

As in the case of the preceding game, we forego a description of the process by which we find a winning strategy for A and confine ourselves simply to presenting one such strategy. Note that the ideas depend greatly on the details of the game in question and demand considerable ingenuity and resourcefulness.

6. THE TREE OF A GAME

Our immediate goal consists in finding an algorithm which will give a "best" strategy for every game in a fairly large class. To avoid formal complexities, instead of giving exact definitions of the notions used, we shall sometimes merely explain them and illustrate them by giving examples.

We first note the following properties of the two games described:

1. The game is played by two players who alternately take turns at making a move.

2. The game ends with exactly one of two possible outcomes: (*a*) either A, the player who moves first, wins (this outcome is denoted below by "+"), or (*b*) the other player, B, wins (denoted by "−").

3. Each move consists of a *choice by the player* of one of a set of admissible moves (note that the choice is a decision by the player, rather than the outcome of some chance event such as throwing dice).

4. At any point in the game both players have full information as to what moves have already been made and what moves can be made.

5. There is an upper limit to the number of moves in a play.

In what follows we shall first assume that all the games in question possess properties 1–5.

It is an obvious and trivial fact that the players cannot both simultaneously have a winning strategy. What is less obvious is that in every game there is a winning strategy for one of the players. Before turning to the proof of this assertion we shall show how a game can be given a convenient graphical representation in the form of a *tree*.

The tree corresponding to the following game (a simplified form of the "Eleven matches" game) is illustrated in Fig. 1: There are six matches on a table; each player in turn picks up one or two matches. The loser is the one who picks up the last match.

The *vertices* of the tree represent the various situations which can occur in a play of the game. The *branches* emanating from a vertex represent the possible choices which the player can make.

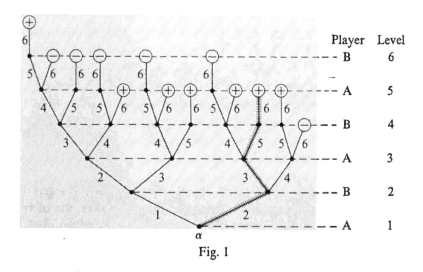

Fig. 1

In our example there are two possibilities for each move (except the last). For definiteness we let the left branch from any vertex correspond to picking up one match and the right branch to picking up two matches. A play of the game corresponds to a broken line joining the bottom vertex α of the tree (the *base* of the tree) to an *end vertex* (that is, a vertex from which no branches emanate). The outcome of the play is marked at each end vertex.

In Fig. 1 each branch is marked with the total number of matches which have been picked up at that stage of the play. The hatched line represents the play

A B A B

2 1 2 1

in which A wins.

We assign a *level* (see Fig. 1) to each vertex other than an end vertex. The highest level occurring in a tree is called the *order* of the tree; it equals the maximum length of a play of the given game (property 5 thus asserts that all games under consideration have a finite order). The vertices of odd level correspond to situations in which it is A's move and those of even level to situations in which it is B's move.

So far we have considered the tree only as some sort of graphical picture of a game whose rules were given beforehand in some other form. However, nothing prevents us from taking a tree as the definition of a game. For example, Fig. 2a defines a game

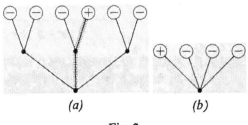

(a)   (b)

Fig. 2

in which every play consists of exactly two moves: A starts by making one of three possible moves and then B makes one of two possible moves. In this game there is only one possible play in which A wins (the hatched broken line). The tree of Fig. 2b defines a game which is played in a single move. For various reasons it will also be useful to speak of "games" of no moves as illustrated in Fig. 3a and 3b. In these "games" neither player does anything; one is just automatically declared the winner.

Every vertex (not an end vertex) can be regarded as the base of a "subtree" of lower order, which itself corresponds to some game.

$\oplus$ $\ominus$

(a)   (b)

Fig. 3

The representation of a game by means of a tree allows one to represent any strategy for A graphically as a system of arrows joining vertices of odd level to vertices of the next higher (even) level. To represent a strategy, a system of arrows must possess the properties:

1. Not more than one arrow starts at any vertex (that is, a strategy for player A must uniquely determine his choice in any given situation).

2. If there is an arrow leading to a vertex γ (of even level), then any adjacent vertex on the next higher level must be the origin of an arrow (Fig. 4). This condition guarantees that the strategy will give a move for A, regardless of what B does. A strategy for B is defined similarly.

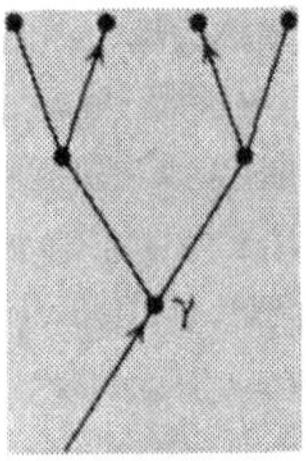

Fig. 4

The strategy for A in the game of "Six matches" in which A always picks exactly one match is illustrated in Fig. 5. This strategy yields 2 plays in which A loses and 2 in which he wins.

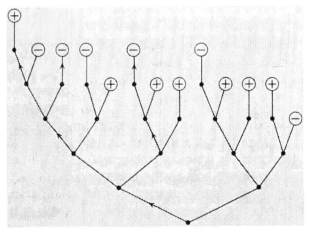

Fig. 5

7. ALGORITHM FOR A WINNING STRATEGY

THEOREM. *In any game satisfying properties 1–5, there is a winning strategy for one of the players.*

The *proof* of this theorem will consist of a description of an algorithm which in any game will yield a winning strategy for one of the players. The algorithm is constructed by induction[1] on v, the length of the longest play possible in the game (v is the order of the tree of the game).

The case of $v = 0$. In this case a play consists of no moves. The trees of the only two games of this kind are illustrated in Fig. 3. The "strategy" of doing nothing (that is, the one represented by no arrows at all) is a winning strategy for A in the game of Fig. 3*a* and for B in the game of Fig. 3*b*. Thus, there is always a winning strategy for one of the players.

The passage from v *to* $v + 1$. Suppose the theorem to have been established for all orders $\leq v$; we shall prove that it also holds for order $v + 1$. In this case the tree of the game has the form represented in Fig. 6, where the triangles represent subtrees whose bases

---

[1] See *The Method of Mathematical Induction* by I. S. Sominskii, published in this series.

are the vertices $\gamma_1, \gamma_2, \ldots, \gamma_n$ adjacent to α, the base of the entire tree. As usual, we let A be the player who has the first move. Then the subtrees $\Delta_1, \Delta_2, \ldots, \Delta_n$ represent games in which B moves first (or games of no moves); moreover, these games are all of order at most ν.

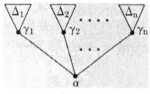

Fig. 6

By the induction hypothesis, the theorem holds for all of them. If A has a winning strategy for any of these games, say Δ_i, then A has a winning strategy for the entire game: it suffices to adjoin the arrow joining α and γ_i to A's winning strategy for Δ_i. If, on the other hand, B has a winning strategy for all of the subgames $\Delta_1, \Delta_2, \ldots, \Delta_n$, then he has a winning strategy for the entire game; he merely combines his winning strategies for the subgames. (That is, his winning strategy will be the collection of all arrows which enter into any of the winning strategies for the subgames.)

The case in which α represents the position of B may be analyzed in exactly the same way.

This concludes the proof and the description of the algorithm. Let us illustrate the process with the "Six matches" game (Fig. 7). First, going from the top of the diagram to the bottom we mark each vertex with a plus sign or minus sign, depending on whether A or B has a winning strategy for the subgame with that vertex as base.

The single non-end vertex of level 6 must be marked with a plus

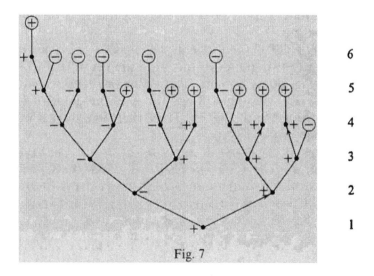

Fig. 7

sign. Now consider the vertices of level 5 from left to right. Recall that it is A's move on this level. It is clear that the leftmost vertex must be marked with a plus sign, since the only adjacent vertex on level 6 is marked with a plus sign. The remaining non-end vertices on level 5 must be marked with minus signs. Among the vertices of level 4 (where it is B's move) we find four minus vertices, namely those adjacent to a minus vertex on level 5, and three plus vertices.

Continuing this process we arrive at level 1, whose single vertex (the base of the tree) must be assigned a plus sign. Thus, A has a winning strategy. We now insert arrows, going from the bottom of the diagram to the top. From the base we draw an arrow to a plus vertex on level 2 (in our example there is only one such vertex). From each vertex on level 3 which is adjacent to the arrowhead we draw an arrow joining it to a plus vertex on level 4. In our example we now have a complete strategy, and the process ends here (Fig. 7). As can be seen from the figure, only two plays are possible when A employs this strategy, and A wins in both.

We observe now that the theorem in this section and the algorithm on which it is based can be generalized to take in *the case where properties 1 and 2 of section 6 are not satisfied* (that is, to a game in which only properties 3, 4, 5 hold). For example, we can consider games between two players A and B in which besides A or B winning it is also possible for the game to end in a tie (for example, tick-tack-toe). Here it may turn out that neither player has a winning strategy; in this case the algorithm will yield for each player a strategy which assures him of at least a tie (or, if the opponent makes an unwise move, even a win).

On the other hand, the game of chess fails to satisfy property 5.[1] Nevertheless, by adding the new rule that a game of, say, 40 moves shall be declared a tie, we obtain a game which does possess properties 3, 4, and 5. Thus, there is a strategy which will assure one of the players of at least a tie. To find it, it is sufficient to construct the tree for chess with a 40-move limit and use the above procedure to find an optimum strategy. If it turns out that there is a winning strategy for white (player A), then the game is predetermined in white's favor, provided that he follows this

[1] This statement is not true if the international tournament rules are followed. For a proof that chess fails to satisfy property 5 when it is played under the old "German rule" that the game is a draw if the same sequence of moves occurs three times in succession, see F. Bagemihl, "Transfinitely Endless Chess," in *Zeitschrift für Mathematische Logik*, Vol. 2 (1956), pp. 215–17.

strategy strictly. Similarly, the outcome of the game would also be predetermined if black had a winning strategy or if both players had a tying strategy. Thus, the application to chess of the algorithm considered above must lead to a complete analysis of the game such as we were able to make for the "Six matches" game.

Why does chess, nonetheless, remain a game which demands great skill and ingenuity? Here we have encountered the *practical infeasibility* of the process prescribed by the algorithm. Twenty branches (one for each of the possible first moves for white) emanate from the base of the tree for chess. The number of branches from each of the higher-level vertices is also generally very large. The order of the tree is, thus, very large. Nevertheless, we must give an affirmative answer to the question of whether we have an exact list of instructions which enables us to find the optimum strategy for any game of the class under consideration (in a finite number of steps, of course). Thus, the method prescribed by this list of instructions is *potentially feasible,* but not *practically feasible,* because of the large number of operations required.

Just how practical it is to apply the preceding method to a given game depends on the complexity of the game, the speed at which we can perform the operations involved, and the amount of time we are willing to spend on it. We are, of course, interested chiefly in processes which are *practically feasible.* However, there is no precise mathematical criterion for distinguishing between practical and impractical processes. Practicality depends on the means available for computation, and this can change, for example, with the development of technology. Thus, with the advent of the high-speed computing machine, many hitherto infeasible processes have become realizable in practice.

However cumbersome the algorithm considered above may be, its existence is a noteworthy fact. For up to now *no algorithm whatever* has been found for Hilbert's problem on Diophantine equations! Meanwhile, the discovery of an algorithm, even a cumbersome one, can give hope that it may be simplified or that a more convenient algorithm may be constructed.

By virtue of the above considerations, whenever we speak of a computational process or, in general, of a process prescribed by some algorithm, we shall always mean simply a process which would give the desired result were it carried out, even if present computational methods are not sufficient to do this in practice.

3. An Algorithm for Finding Paths in a Labyrinth

8. LABYRINTHS

Greek mythology tells of the hero Theseus, who entered a labyrinth in order to find and kill the monstrous Minotaur. He was helped by Ariadne, who gave him a ball of thread, one end of which she held. Theseus unwound the thread as he went deeper into the labyrinth, then by rewinding the thread found his way safely out again.

Reminiscent of this ancient legend is the modern "Mouse in the Labyrinth" device of the American mathematician and engineer Claude Shannon.[1] The "mouse" is placed at one position of a special labyrinth and another object which we might call a "piece of cheese" is placed at another position. The mouse wanders through the labyrinth in circuitous paths until it finds the "cheese." If it is then put into the same starting position, it will go straight to the "cheese" without any aimless wandering. (The "mouse" is electromagnetically controlled by a relay circuit which records the "successful" turns in the first attempt, so that on the second trip the "mouse" makes only these.)

We shall consider here a related problem of finding a path through a labyrinth (or, more correctly, a class of such problems), and we shall develop an algorithm which solves this class of problems.

We may think of the labyrinth as a finite system of junctions, from which corridors emanate. Each corridor joins two junctions (which are then said to be *adjacent*). There may also be "dead-end" junctions, from which only one corridor leads away. The labyrinth may be represented geometrically by a system of points $A, B, C, \ldots$ (the junctions) and line segments $AB, BC, \ldots$ (the corridors), each segment connecting a pair of the points (Fig. 8).

---

[1] C. E. Shannon. "Computers and Automata," *Proceedings of the IRE*, Vol. 41 (1953), p. 1234.

We say that a junction Y is *accessible* from a junction X if there is a path leading from X to Y through some sequence of inter-

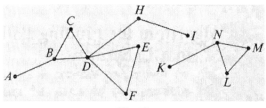

Fig. 8

mediate corridors. More precisely, this means that either X and Y are adjacent or there is some sequence X_1, X_2, X_3, ... X_n of junctions such that X and X_1, X_1 and X_2, X_2 and X_3, ..., and finally, X_n and Y are adjacent. For example, in Fig. 8, H is accessible from A via the path AB, BC, CD, DE, EF, FD, DH, while K is not accessible from A. Furthermore, if Y is accessible from X at all, then it is accessible via some *simple path*, by which we mean a path which passes through no junction (and *a fortiori* no corridor) more than once (although there may, of course, be junctions or corridors through which it does not pass at all). In the last example the path was not simple, but by removing the loop DE, EF, FD, we obtain the simple path AB, BC, CD, DH.

Suppose that the Minotaur is at some junction M of the labyrinth and that Theseus sets out to hunt him from the junction A, where Ariadne is waiting; we must then solve the problem: Is the junction M accessible from the junction A?[1] If so, Theseus must find the Minotaur by whatever path he can and then return to Ariadne by a *simple path*. If not, he must return to Ariadne.

There are innumerable possible labyrinths, and for any given labyrinth there will be several possibilities for the locations of A and M with respect to each other. Since at the beginning Theseus knows neither the structure of the labyrinth nor the location of the Minotaur, the solution of the problem must be in the form of a general search method which can be used in any labyrinth and for any relative position of A and M with respect to each other. In other words, the solution must be an algorithm for solving any problem of the given type.

[1] It is natural to assume that $A \neq M$.

9. THE LABYRINTH ALGORITHM

In order to construct such an algorithm, we prescribe a special method of searching. At each step of the search we can separate the corridors into three classes: those through which Theseus has never passed (we shall call these *green* corridors), those through which he has passed once (*yellow*), and those through which he has passed twice (*red*). Furthermore, from any junction Theseus may move to an adjacent junction in one of two ways:

1. *Unwinding the thread.* Theseus moves along any green corridor to an adjacent junction, unwinding Ariadne's thread as he goes; this corridor is then considered yellow.

2. *Rewinding the thread.* Theseus returns along a yellow corridor to an adjacent junction, rewinding Ariadne's thread as he goes; this corridor is then considered red.

Note that Theseus is not allowed to go through a red corridor. We assume that Theseus makes some mark by which he can later distinguish a green corridor from a red one. He can distinguish the yellow corridors because they have Ariadne's thread stretched along them. The choice of each move depends upon the conditions which Theseus finds at the junction where he happens to be. These conditions will be one or more of the following:

1. *Minotaur.* The Minotaur is discovered at the given junction.

2. *Loop.* Ariadne's thread already passes through the given junction; in other words, there are at least two other yellow corridors leading from the junction.

3. *Green.* There is at least one green corridor leading from the junction.

4. *Ariadne.* Ariadne is at the given junction.

5. *Fifth case.* None of the above conditions prevails.

Our search method may now be described by means of the following table.

Condition	Move
1. Minotaur	Stop
2. Loop	Rewind the thread
3. Green	Unwind the thread
4. Ariadne	Stop
5. Fifth case	Rewind the thread

19

Finding himself at any junction Theseus decides his next move as follows: Beginning with condition 1, he checks the left-hand column of the preceding table in numerical order until he finds a condition which prevails at the junction. He then performs the corresponding move in the right-hand column. He continues to move in this way until he comes to a "Stop" order.

That this method works is a direct consequence of the following three assertions.

1. For A and M located anywhere in the labyrinth Theseus must eventually come to a "Stop" order, either at A or at M, after a finite number of moves.

2. If the "Stop" order comes at M, then the Minotaur is accessible. Moreover, Ariadne's thread will be stretched along a simple path from A to M; by rewinding the thread, Theseus can return to Ariadne along this path.

3. If the "Stop" order comes at A, then the Minotaur is *inaccessible*.

Before proving these assertions, we shall give two examples of the use of the method.

EXAMPLE 1. Suppose that the search begins at junction A of the labyrinth (Fig. 8) and that the Minotaur is at junction F. One search following our method is given in Table 1. (Since the choice of which green corridor to traverse is arbitrary, there will naturally be other possible search patterns.)

TABLE 1

Move No.	Condition found by Theseus at the junction	Move	Corridor chosen	State of corridor after move
1	Green	Unwind	AB	Yellow
2	,,	,,	BC	,,
3	,,	,,	CD	,,
4	,,	,,	DH	,,
5	,,	,,	HI	,,
6	Fifth case	Rewind	IH	Red
7	,, ,,	,,	HD	,,
8	Green	Unwind	DB	Yellow
9	Loop	Rewind	BD	Red
10	Green	Unwind	DF	Yellow
11	Minotaur	Stop	. . . .	. . . .

We see that in this example the Minotaur is accessible. If we now pick out from the last two columns the corridors which end up yellow, we find the following simple path leading from A to F: AB, BC, CD, DF.

EXAMPLE 2. If the search begins at junction K of Fig. 8, with the Minotaur still at F, we get a search pattern such as that of Table 2. In this case the Minotaur is inaccessible.

TABLE 2

Move No.	Condition found by Theseus at the Junction	Move	Corridor chosen	State of corridor after move
1	Green	Unwind	KN	Yellow
2	,,	,,	NL	,,
3	,,	,,	LM	,,
4	,,	,,	MN	,,
5	Loop	Rewind	NM	Red
6	Fifth Case	,,	ML	,,
7	,, ,,	,,	LN	,,
8	,, ,,	,,	NK	,,
9	Ariadne	Stop	....	......

10. PROOF OF THE LABYRINTH ALGORITHM

We now prove assertions 1–3 stated on page 20.

Proof of assertion 1. We first prove by induction on the number of moves made by Theseus that at each stage of the search one and only one of the following conditions holds:

(*a*) There are no yellow corridors in the labyrinth, and Theseus is at junction A (Ariadne).

(*b*) There are one or more yellow corridors in the labyrinth, and the yellow corridors, in the same order in which Theseus passed through them, form a path leading from A to the present position of Theseus.

Furthermore, it will be found that Theseus never passes through a red corridor.

Obviously, exactly one of the alternatives (*a*) and (*b*) holds when Theseus makes his first move; he is then at A and all corridors

21

are green. We now assume that one of the alternatives holds after the $(n-1)$st move and must prove that one must also hold after the nth move (provided, of course, that the $(n-1)$st move did not lead to a stop order).

First suppose that after the $(n-1)$st move alternative (a) holds. Then the next move must be either from A to some adjacent junction K along a green corridor (so that after the nth move we have case (b) with only one yellow corridor, AK), or a stop (so that after the nth move we have case (a)).

Next suppose that after the $(n-1)$st move alternative (b) holds, and that there are s yellow corridors, forming the path $AA_1, A_1A_2,$ $\ldots, A_{s-1}K$. The choice of the nth move depends on conditions at the junction K; the possibilities are:

1. *Minotaur.* The nth move is a stop at the junction K, leaving the same yellow corridors (case (b) after the nth move).

2. *Loop.* Theseus rewinds the thread along the yellow corridor KA_{s-1}, which then becomes red. The yellow path becomes one corridor shorter. If the number s of yellow corridors was greater than one, we have case (b) after the nth move, with $s-1$ yellow corridors; if s was one, we have case (a).

3. *Green.* Theseus unwinds the thread along some green corridor, which becomes yellow. We then have case (b), with $s+1$ yellow corridors.

4. *Ariadne.* Theseus will never act on this alternative, since if $K=A$, the loop condition, which takes precedence over this one, will also hold.

5. *Fifth case.* If none of the first four conditions holds, Theseus will rewind the thread. Just as for the loop condition, this leads to (a) if $s=1$ and to (b) if $s>1$.

We have now established that one of the alternatives (a) and (b) must hold. It is clear that Theseus passes through no corridor more than twice, since he never passes through a red corridor. Since the number of corridors is finite, the procedure must eventually come to a stop; thus, the final move must be to the junction where either the Minotaur or Ariadne is.

Proof of assertion 2. If the stop order comes at the Minotaur's junction, then the Minotaur is obviously accessible. Also, Ariadne's thread forms a path back to the starting point along yellow corridors, as we have just shown. That this is a simple path follows from the fact that every time Theseus completed a loop, he rewound the thread, thus eliminating the loop.

22

Proof of assertion 3. In the case of a stop at Ariadne's junction, first note that:

(*a*) Every corridor of the labyrinth has been traversed either twice (a red corridor) or not at all (a green corridor); in other words, there are no yellow corridors in the labyrinth, and the thread is completely rewound (for otherwise the loop condition would hold and there would be no stop).

(*b*) All corridors leading from the junction A are red, since if one were green, Theseus would have traversed it rather than stopping, since "Green" is ahead of "Ariadne" on the list.

Assume now that assertion 3 is not true, that the Minotaur is accessible via some path $AA_1, A_1A_2, \ldots A_nM$. The first corridor in this path must be red, since it leads from A, and the last corridor must be green, since Theseus did not reach the Minotaur. Let A_iA_{i+1} be the first green corridor of the path. This means that there are a green and a red corridor leading from A_i. Now consider the last time that Theseus passed through the junction A_i. He must have left along one of the now red corridors leading from A_i by rewinding the thread, which means that he must have encountered either condition 2 (loop) or condition 5. But it could not have been 5, since there is a green corridor A_iA_{i+1} leading from A_i; therefore, it must have been a loop. But this immediately leads to a contradiction by the following argument: If he had found a loop at A_i the last time, there would have been at least two yellow corridors leading from it; he would then have left along one of them, making it red, but leaving at least one still yellow. But we have seen that no yellow corridors are left at the end of the search, which means that Theseus must have passed through the rest of the yellow corridors leading from A_i later, and thus passed through A_i again, which contradicts our assumption that this was the last time he passed through A_i. This proves assertion 3.

In this search method there is an element of chance. For condition 3 (green), the next move is not uniquely specified; if there are several green corridors leading from the junction, any one of them may be taken next. This violates the deterministic property which we spoke of in the last section as being inherent in all algorithms. This element of chance can easily be eliminated, however, and a true algorithm obtained. If there are several green corridors leading from a given junction, we simply decide on a convention for choosing one of them; for example, we always choose the first corridor in a clockwise direction from the one by which Theseus entered the junction. The analysis of such questions, involving chance acts, is of great theoretical and practical importance, particularly in game theory and its applications to economics.

Specifications of precisely this kind give the "best" strategy (in a certain sense) for an extensive class of games in which the choice of moves depends not only on decisions by the players, but also on random choices. Such instruction lists are a direct generalization of the algorithms described in the preceding section for games without random choices. But we shall not touch on this question and shall not consider instruction lists involving random choices to be algorithms. The strict determinacy of an algorithm and the uniqueness of the course of the process which it specifies are its essential features.

Returning to the algorithm in question (after eliminating the element of chance), one should note that simpler search methods can be given for labyrinths of a more particular form. At the same time, it seems natural to suppose that for the general case of an arbitrary labyrinth, an algorithm cannot be other than some kind of sorting-out procedure. Therefore, it is doubtful that an algorithm simpler than the one we have given can be constructed.

4. The Word Problem

The *word problem* is a further generalization of Theseus' search. Whereas Theseus' search may be carried out in an arbitrary finite labyrinth, the word problem is in a certain sense a search in an infinite labyrinth. The problem arises in the branches of modern algebra known as the *theory of associative systems* and the *theory of groups,* although it goes beyond the framework of these theories. Different versions of this problem have been studied with successful results by two Soviet mathematicians, A. A. Markov and P. S. Novikov, and their students.

11. ASSOCIATIVE CALCULI

We first introduce some preliminary concepts. By an *alphabet* we mean any finite set of distinct symbols; each of these symbols is called a *letter* of the alphabet. For instance, $\{\alpha, \text{ц}, z, ?\}$ is an alphabet made up of the following letters: Greek α, Russian ц, Latin z, and the question mark. A *word* in a given alphabet is any sequence of letters from the alphabet. For example, *abaa* and *bbac* are words in the alphabet $\{a, b, c\}$. If a word L is part of another word M, we shall speak of the *occurrence* of L in M. Thus, in the word *abcbcbab* there are two occurrences of the word *bcb*—one beginning with the second letter, the other with the fourth. We shall consider transformations of one word into another by means of certain *admissible substitutions* and shall write these in the form

$$P - Q \quad \text{or} \quad P \to Q,$$

where P and Q are two words in the same alphabet.

The application of the *directed substitution* $P \to Q$ in a word R is possible only when P occurs in R; it consists of substituting Q for one of the occurrences of P in R. The application of the *undirected substitution* $P - Q$ consists of either substituting P for an occurrence of Q or substituting Q for an occurrence of P. From now on we shall be concerned mainly with undirected substitutions and shall refer to them simply as substitutions where no misunderstanding can arise.

EXAMPLE. The substitution $ab - bcb$ can be applied to the word $abcbcbab$ in four ways: substituting for each of the two occurrences of bcb gives the words

$$a \underline{ab} cbab \quad \text{and} \quad abc \underline{ab} ab,$$

and substituting for each of the two occurrences of ab gives

$$\underline{bcb} cbcbab \quad \text{and} \quad abcbcb \underline{bcb}.$$

This substitution cannot be applied to the word $bacb$.

We define an *associative calculus* as the totality of words in some alphabet, together with some finite set of admissible substitutions.

In order to specify an associative calculus, it is sufficient to give the alphabet and the set of admissible substitutions.

12. THE WORD EQUIVALENCE PROBLEM

If a word R can be transformed into a word S by a single application of an admissible substitution, we say that R is *adjacent* to S. Note that if R is adjacent to S, then S is adjacent to R. A sequence of words

$$R_1, R_2, \ldots, R_{n-1}, R_n$$

such that R_1 is adjacent to R_2, R_2 to $R_3, \ldots$, and R_{n-1} to R_n will be called a *deductive chain* from R_1 to R_n. If there is a deductive chain from the word R to the word S, then there is, of course, also a deductive chain from S to R; in this case we say that R and S are *equivalent* and denote this fact by $R \sim S$. It is clear that if $R \sim S$ and $S \sim T$, then $R \sim T$. Later we shall make use of the following theorem.

THEOREM. *Suppose that $P \sim Q$; then if P occurs in a word R, the application of the substitution $P \to Q$ in R yields a word which is equivalent to R.*

Proof. R can be written in the form SPT, where S is that part of R which precedes the occurrence of P, and T is that part which follows it. Then the transformed word is SQT. Since $P \sim Q$, there exists a deductive chain

$$P, P_1, \ldots, P_m, Q.$$

Then, as is easily seen, the sequence of words

$$SPT, SP_1T, \ldots, SP_mT, SQT$$

is a deductive chain from SPT (that is, from R) to the transformed word SQT. Thus, the theorem is proved.

EXAMPLE. Consider the following associative calculus:
Alphabet:

$$\{a, b, c, d, e\}$$

Admissible substitutions:

$ac \longrightarrow ca$	$abac \longrightarrow abacc$
$ad \longrightarrow da$	$eca \longrightarrow ae$
$bc \longrightarrow cb$	$edb \longrightarrow be$
$bd \longrightarrow db$	

In this calculus only the third substitution is applicable to the word $abcde$, so that the only word adjacent to it is $acbde$. Moreover, $abcde \sim cadedb$, which can be seen from the deductive chain

$$a\underline{bc}de, \ ac\underline{bd}e, \ ca\underline{bd}e, \ cad\underline{be}, \ cadedb.$$

None of the transformations is applicable to the word $aaabb$; so there are no words adjacent to it. This means, in particular, that no other word can be equivalent to it.

Every associative calculus has its *word equivalence problem:*
Given any two words in the calculus, determine whether or not they are equivalent.

Since the number of possible words in any calculus is infinite, each calculus has an infinite number of problems of this type. However, we hope to find a solution in the form of an algorithm for determining the equivalence or nonequivalence of *any pair* of words.

It may seem that the word problem is just an artificial puzzle and that finding an algorithm for it is of no real interest. But this is far from the truth—the problem arises quite naturally and is of great theoretical and practical importance, fully justifying the effort spent in finding an algorithm. However, we shall defer discussion of these questions for now and proceed to a consideration of other facts.

13. WORD PROBLEMS AND LABYRINTHS

We can show a relation between the word-equivalence problem and the problem of Theseus as follows: If we construct a "junction" for every word and a "corridor" joining each pair of junctions representing two adjacent words, then we can represent any associative calculus by a labyrinth having an infinite number of junctions and corridors. Since only a finite number of substitutions are admissible, each junction will have only a finite number of corridors leading from it, and there may even be junctions with no corridors (for example, the word *aaabb* in the example in this section). A deductive chain leading from a word *R* to a word *S* is represented by a path in the labyrinth leading from one junction to the other, which means that the equivalence of words corresponds to the accessibility of one junction from another. Thus, in this representation the word problem becomes a search problem in an infinite labyrinth.

In order to see better some of the difficulties which arise, consider first the *restricted word problem:*

For any two words R and T in a given associative calculus, determine whether or not one can be transformed into the other by a chain of not more than k admissible substitutions (where *k* is an arbitrary but fixed positive integer).

It is easy to construct an algorithm for this problem, namely, a sorting-out algorithm such as we could have used in the labyrinth problem. Write down the word *R*, then all words adjacent to *R*, then all words adjacent to these, and so on, *k* times. Then asking whether or not *R* can be transformed into *T* using no more than *k* substitutions is the same as asking whether or not the word *T* appears in this list.

If we go back to the *unrestricted word problem*, the situation is quite different. Since a deductive chain leading from *R* to *T* may turn out to be of any length (if it exists at all), in general we have no way of knowing when to stop the sorting-out process. For example, suppose that we have already repeated the procedure $10^{20} = 100,000,000,000,000,000,000$ times, and thus have a list of all the words into which *R* can be transformed by means of 1, 2, 3, ..., or 10^{20} admissible substitutions, and suppose further that *T* does not appear in this list. Can we say that *T* is not equivalent to *R*? The answer, of course, is that we cannot, since there is still the possibility that *R* and *T* are equivalent, but that the shortest deductive chain connecting them has more than 10^{20} steps. (As an exercise, the reader may construct a calculus which has a pair of words which are equivalent but are connected by no deductive chain of length 10^{20} or less.)

14. CONSTRUCTION OF ALGORITHMS

To obtain an algorithm we must abandon the idea of a simple sorting and instead look for other ideas, based upon analysis of the transformation mechanism itself. For instance, take the problem of the equivalence of the words *abaacd* and *acbdad* in the calculus of the Example of section 12. We can prove that these words are not equivalent as follows: In each of the admissible substitutions, each side contains the same number of *a*'s. Therefore, in any deductive chain in this calculus, each word must have the same number of occurrences of *a*. Since the number of occurrences of *a* in the words *abaacd* and *acbdad* is not the same, these words cannot belong to a common deductive chain, and are therefore not equivalent.

Such a property, which is common to all members of a deductive chain, is called a *deductive invariant*. A deductive invariant may aid us in finding an algorithm.

EXAMPLE 1. Consider the following associative calculus:
Alphabet:

$$\{a, b, c, d, e\}$$

Admissible substitutions:

ab — ba	ae — ea	be — eb	de — ed
ac — ca	bc — cb	cd — dc	
ad — da	bd — db	ce — ec	

Here the admissible substitutions do not affect what letters are present in a word, but only their order. It is not hard to show that two words are equivalent if and only if each contains the same number of occurrences of every letter as does the other. We thus have a simple algorithm for determining equivalence in this case: Count the number of occurrences of each letter in each word, and compare the results.

We now introduce a generalization of the concepts of "word" and "admissible substitution." In addition to ordinary words in a given alphabet, we shall admit the *empty word,* which contains no letters and is denoted by $\wedge$. We also allow substitutions of the form

$$P - \wedge.$$

The substitution of $\wedge$ for P means simply that if there is an occurrence of P in a word R, we delete it entirely; the substitution of P for $\wedge$ means that P may be introduced into the word R at any point—before the first letter of R, or between two letters of R, or after the last letter of R.

We now consider the following:

EXAMPLE 2. Given the associative calculus with alphabet $\{a, b, c\}$ and with the set of admissible substitutions:

$b \longrightarrow acc$	$bb \longrightarrow \wedge$
$ca \longrightarrow accc$	$cccc \longrightarrow \wedge$
$aa \longrightarrow \wedge$	

find an algorithm for the word equivalence problem in this calculus.

We first construct an auxiliary algorithm—the *reduction algorithm.* This is an algorithm for transforming any word into an equivalent word of a particular form—its *reduced word.*

Consider the following *ordered* system of *directed* substitutions:

$b \longrightarrow acc$	$aa \longrightarrow \wedge$
$ca \longrightarrow accc$	$cccc \longrightarrow \wedge$

Given any word R, find the first directed substitution in the list which is applicable to it and perform the substitution at the first possible application point from the left. This gives an equivalent word R'. Find the first substitution in the list which can be applied to R' and apply it. After a finite number of substitutions we obtain a word S to which none of the transformations can be applied; we say that *the algorithm reduces the word R to the word S.*[1]

---

[1] Algorithms such as this one for transforming words in a given alphabet according to some ordered set of directed substitutions are called *normal algorithms.* The theory of normal algorithms, which are of great theoretical and practical interest, was developed by A. A. Markov and is presented in his book *Theory of Algorithms,* a translation of which is available from the Office of Technical Services, U. S. Department of Commerce, Washington 25, D. C., OTS accession number 60-51085.

We can show that the reduction algorithm transforms any word R into one of these eight words (the reduced words):

$$\wedge, \, c, \, cc, \, ccc, \, a, \, ac, \, acc, \, accc.$$

1. If the letter b appears in the word R, then successive applications of the first directed substitution will change each occurrence of b into acc, until no b remains; since b does not appear in any other substitutions, it cannot appear in any reduced word.

2. The letter a cannot appear directly to the right of the letter c in any reduced word, since the second directed substitution changes every occurrence of ca into $accc$.

3. There cannot be two consecutive a's in any reduced word, because of the third substitution.

4. The letter c cannot appear more than three times in a row because of the last substitution.

The above list of eight words therefore includes all the reduced words, since according to the discussion given above, a reduced word can consist of at most one a followed by at most three c's.

Clearly, every word is equivalent to its reduced word; therefore, two words are equivalent if and only if their reduced words are either the same or equivalent. But we shall prove shortly that no two of the eight reduced words listed above are equivalent. It follows that two words are equivalent if and only if they reduce to the same word. From this we can construct an algorithm for the word problem: *Apply the reduction algorithm to each of the two words being examined, and compare the results obtained; if the results coincide, then the original words are equivalent; otherwise they are not equivalent.*

Suppose, for example, we are given the words *cacb* and *bb*. First find the reduced words:

(1) *cacb, cacacc, accccacc, acccacccc, accacccccc,*

   acacccccccccc, aacccccccccccccc, ccccccccccccccc,

   ccccccccc, ccccc, cc.

(2) *bb, accb, accacc, acacccc, aaccccccc, ccccccc, cccc,* $\wedge$.

Result. The words *cacb* and *bb* are not equivalent, since their reduced words *cc* and $\wedge$ are different.[1]

---

[1] The fact that the reduced word of *bb* is $\wedge$ shows that the substitution *bb* — $\wedge$ in our original list was superfluous, which explains why we omitted it from the reduction algorithm.

Proof that no two of the eight reduced words are equivalent. In the first place, if there is a deductive chain connecting two words R and S, neither of which contains the letter b, then it is possible to construct a deductive chain connecting them such that none of the words in the chain contains the letter b. We do this by taking every word in the given deductive chain and substituting in it the word acc for every occurrence of the letter b. This gives us a sequence of words in which every two consecutive words are either adjacent (in the sense of the calculus) or identical. If we now delete every word which coincides with the preceding word, we are left with a deductive chain. Furthermore, the substitution $b - acc$ is not used in the chain.

Next, note that the evenness or oddness of the number of occurrences of the letter a is the same on both sides of every admissible substitution. The same is true also of the letter c. This means that the *parity* (that is, "evenness" or "oddness") of the number of occurrences of a (or c) is a deductive invariant for any deductive chain of this type. It follows at once that none of the four reduced words that contain one occurrence of a is equivalent to any of the four reduced words that contain no a's. Similarly, none of the four reduced words that contain one or three c's is equivalent to any of the four that contain no or two c's. Therefore, we have now only to establish the nonequivalence of the following four pairs of words:

$$\wedge, cc; \quad c, ccc; \quad a, acc; \quad ac, accc.$$

If any of the first three pairs are equivalent, then it would follow from the theorem we proved earlier (p. 26) that the fourth pair is also equivalent. Thus, it is sufficient to establish nonequivalence merely for the fourth pair: ac, $accc$.

We first define some terms. By the *index of an occurrence* of a in a word R we mean the number of occurrences of c in the word to the right of the given occurrence of a. By the *index of the word* R we mean the sum of the indices of all occurrences of a in R.[1] Neither of the substitutions $aa - \wedge$ and $cccc - \wedge$ changes the parity of the index of a word. If aa is substituted for the empty word, the index of the word is increased by the sum of the indices of the two occurrences of a. But both these indices must be the same, which

[1] For example, in the word $acbca$ the index of the first occurrence of a is 2 and the index of the second occurrence of a is 0. The index of the word is $2 + 0 = 2$.

means that the index of the word is increased by an even number and thus its parity is unchanged. Similarly, if the empty word is substituted for *aa*, the index of the word is reduced by an even number.

In inserting *cccc* the indices of some occurrences of *a* are raised by 4, and the others remain the same; thus, the index of the word is increased by a multiple of 4. The deletion of *cccc* has a similar effect.

Finally, the substitution *ca* — *accc* changes the parity of the index of any word. To show this, we compare the words

$$PcaQ \quad \text{and} \quad PacccQ.$$

The index of every occurrence of *a* in the part *P* of the word is changed by 2 and the index of every occurrence of *a* in the part *Q* remains unchanged. The index of the single occurrence of *a* between *P* and *Q* is changed by 3. Thus, the total index of the word is changed by an odd number, so that its parity is changed.

Now the words *ac* and *accc* have indices of the same parity (1 and 3—both odd). Therefore, if they are equivalent, then any deductive chain connecting them must involve an even number of substitutions *ca* — *accc* (we may restrict ourselves to chains with no occurrences of *b*, as mentioned earlier).

But this condition leads to a contradiction. Each application of the substitution *ca* — *accc* changes the number of occurrences of *c* by 2, so that an even number of applications changes the number of occurrences of *c* by a multiple of 4. Clearly, the substitution *cccc* — $\wedge$ changes the number of occurrences of *c* by 4, and the substitution *aa* — $\wedge$ does not change the number of occurrences of *c* at all. From what we have said, we can conclude that if *ac* and *accc* are equivalent, then the number of occurrences of *c* in them must differ by a multiple of 4, which is not true. Therefore, *ac* and *accc* are not equivalent, which means that, as claimed, none of the reduced words are equivalent.

The detailed solution of the word problem in Example 2 illustrates in many respects the concepts and methods which are used in general. It still remains to demonstrate the relevance and importance of this problem to modern algebra. We shall do so by considering a specific example in the next section.

15. AUTOMORPHISMS OF A SQUARE

Take any square (Fig. 9*I*). Consider the following three *auto-morphisms* (that is, transformations which transform the square into itself):

(1) mirror reflection in a vertical axis passing through the center *O*;

(2) mirror reflection in a horizontal axis passing through the center *O*;

(3) clockwise rotation through 90° about the center *O*. We shall

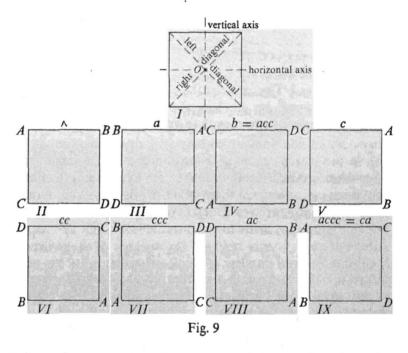

Fig. 9

call these *elementary transformations* and denote them by *a*, *b*, and *c*, respectively. Parts *III*, *IV*, and *V* of Fig. 9 show how the vertices of the square of Fig. 9*II* are changed under each of the elementary transformations.

Under a succession of two or more elementary transformations, the square is also transformed into itself. We shall adopt the customary definition that the *multiplication* of two transformations shall mean their successive application. We shall also employ the usual notation for multiplication and use the word *product* for the resulting transformation. For example, the product *cc* is the result of two successive rotations through 90°, that is, a rotation through 180°.

The product ac is a reflection about the vertical axis followed by a rotation through 90°, which is the same as a reflection about the right diagonal (see Fig. 9I). The product $(ac)(cc)$ of these two transformations is the same as a reflection about the left diagonal.

Our multiplication is not commutative; that is, it makes a difference in which order we multiply two transformations: Fig. 9VIII and 9IX illustrate the arrangement of the vertices of the original square of Fig. 9II after the transformations ac and ca; we can see that they are different. However, our multiplication, like ordinary multiplication, is associative; that is, for any transformations p, q, and r, we have the identity $(pq)r = p(qr)$. Thanks to this, we can ignore the parentheses in any product. For example, $(ac)(cc)$, $(((ac)c)c)$, and $accc$ all represent the same transformation (reflection about the left diagonal).

In what follows, we shall be interested in the set consisting of the three elementary transformations a, b, and c and all transformations which can be represented as products of a finite but arbitrary number of elementary transformations. Because of the associativity of our multiplication, we can omit parentheses and represent these product transformations simply by writing down the elementary transformations in the proper order, for example, abb, $cabb$, $accc$. That is to say, we can represent them as words in the alphabet $\{a, b, c\}$.

It also follows from the associative character of our multiplication that if the words P and Q are written so as to form a single word PQ, then PQ represents a transformation which is the product of the transformations represented by P and Q. For instance, the word $abccab$ represents the product of the transformations represented by abc and cab (or by ab and $ccab$, etc.).

It is clear that there are infinitely many words in the alphabet $\{a, b, c\}$, but it may happen that two different words represent the same transformation. In this case it is natural to say that the words are *equal* and to use the usual notation for equality. The reader can easily verify the equalities

$$b = acc, \tag{1}$$

$$ca = accc. \tag{2}$$

To prove these, just apply the transformations on each side of the equation to the same square, and compare the resulting squares.

Also, it is easy to see that each of the words *aa, bb, cccc* represents the same transformation; it is called the *identity* transformation, since it leaves the vertices of the square in their original positions. Since nothing is really changed by this transformation, we represent it by the empty word $\wedge$. (We leave it to the reader to verify that this convention does not alter the previous assertion.) Thus,

$$aa = \wedge, \tag{3}$$
$$bb = \wedge, \tag{4}$$
$$cccc = \wedge. \tag{5}$$

Comparison of equalities (1)–(5) with the admissible substitutions in the associative calculus of Example 2 of section 14 leads to the following statement, which establishes a connection between that calculus and the transformations of a square:

Two products of the elementary transformations of a square are equal if and only if the words which represent them are equivalent in the calculus of Example 2 of section 14.

It follows from equations (1)–(5) that the application of any admissible substitution to an arbitrary word S produces an equal word. For example, the application of the substitution $ca - accc$ to the word *bcac* gives the word *bacccc*; but since multiplication is associative, we can write $bcac = b(ca)c$ and $bacccc = b(accc)c$. The right sides of these two equations are equal, since they are products of equal factors, which means that the left sides must also be equal. Thus, *any two adjacent words are equal.*

It is now simple to show that if two words are equivalent in our associative calculus, then the corresponding transformations are equal. If $S \sim T$, then in the corresponding deductive chain every two adjacent elements are equal, and therefore $S = T$.

The converse is also true: *if two words are equal, they are equivalent.* If two words are equal, then their reduced words are also equal. (This follows from the statement just proved.) But no two of the reduced words are equal; this may be seen in Fig. 9*II*–*IX*, showing the results of the application to the square of Fig. 9*II* of the transformations corresponding to the reduced words. Thus, if two words are equal, their reduced words must be the same, which means that the words are equivalent.

We have given a concrete geometric meaning to the purely formal idea of equivalence and replaced the determination of equivalence by the solution of a concrete geometric problem. In addition, the algorithm just derived now appears as a general method for solving geometric problems of this type. The situation is similar in other calculi, where a formal equivalence problem may have specific geometric, algebraic, or other interpretations. We can say without exaggeration that there are theorems in every branch of mathematics which can be formulated as a statement concerning the equivalence of two words in some calculus. We shall discuss this further later on (see section 25).

We point out in closing that, having given the calculus of Example 2 of section 14 a geometric interpretation, we can now construct an algorithm directly and even somewhat more simply. For, to test the equivalence of two words in that calculus, it is sufficient to draw the corresponding transformations of a square and to compare the resulting squares.

PROBLEM. Solve the word problem for the associative calculus defined by the alphabet $\{a, b\}$ and the admissible substitutions

$$aaa = bb,$$
$$bbbb = \wedge.$$

37

5. Computing Machines with Automatic Control

16. HUMAN COMPUTATION

Since an algorithm, especially a practical one, is usually based on subtle and complicated arguments, constructing algorithms requires a high degree of ingenuity. But once an algorithm is found, it can be used by a person who does not even know its purpose. He need only be able to perform the few elementary operations required by the algorithm and to follow the directions exactly as given. Proceeding quite mechanically, he can solve any problem of the type for which the algorithm is designed. We might say that such a person acts "like a machine"; we say it figuratively, of course, referring to the deterministic nature of the algorithm, but with the advance of science and technology, the phrase has acquired a literal significance. In place of our hypothetical person, who does not understand (or does not want to know) what he is doing as he solves problems, it is now possible to use a machine. Such is the modern computing machine with automatic control.

Our task will be to describe the basic principles of the construction and operation of such machines.

First, we shall examine the algorithmic process as performed by a human calculator. In following an algorithm, a calculator receives, processes, and stores various data (or *information*). Usually he writes them down (*represents* them) on paper, using numerals, letters, and other symbols. We call such a group of symbols an *alphabet*. For example, in algebra we use an alphabet containing the usual letters, numerals, signs for arithmetic operations, parentheses, etc.

A calculation carried out manually involves the following three factors (see Fig. 10a).

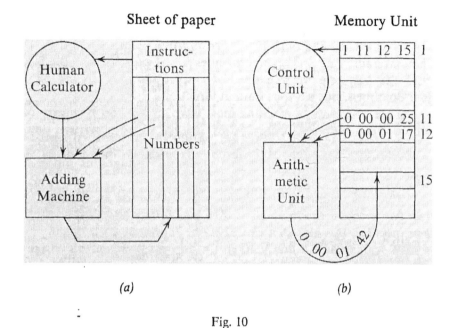

Sheet of paper   Memory Unit

(a)   (b)

Fig. 10

1. The *storage of information* is usually accomplished by writing down all data, including the instructions for solving the problem (the algorithm), on a piece of paper. In practice, of course, the calculator does not write down everything. Some things he remembers (stores in his brain rather than on paper), while some he looks up in charts or tables. However, this must not obscure the basic fact that *some* means is provided for storing all necessary information. Thus, the piece of paper in our figure must be understood to represent *all* ways of storing information.

2. *Processing the information* means performing the elementary operations required by the algorithm. This may be done by using mechanical devices; for example, arithmetic operations may be done on an adding machine or a slide rule. Each step of the calculation consists in taking certain information (for example, numbers) from the paper, performing a specified operation on it, and recording the result at some definite place on the paper.

3. *Control of the process,* that is, the determination of what step is to be performed next, is carried out by the calculator by referring to his instructions.

39

17. COMPUTING MACHINES

What are the components of a computing machine and how do they interact? The answer to this question is suggested by the fact that the machine must carry out operations such as we have just described, but without human direction.

In the first place, a machine must have an *alphabet* by means of which it can represent information. Instead of using written symbols, a machine represents information by physically distinguishable conditions, such as different electrical voltages or different states of magnetization.

Many considerations make it worthwhile to use an alphabet of just two symbols (a *binary* alphabet), which may be called 0 and 1. For instance, this alphabet can easily be represented electrically by a high voltage and a low voltage (or current flow and no current flow). Further, one must take into account that the simplest logical operations are carried out on variables which can take one of two values: true or false. However, the choice of an alphabet and the method of representing information in it have no bearing on our understanding of the structure and operation of a machine. Therefore we shall not go into further details, other than to point out that the binary alphabet and binary calculations (instead of the more usual decimal system) are usually used in modern machines.

Thus, the information which is put into the machine, as well as that which is produced in the course of the calculation, is in the form of certain physical parameters. In the cases which we are interested in, all information is coded numerically. In particular, the algorithm which the machine must follow is itself coded as some list of numbers. An algorithm written for machine execution is called a *program*. The program is the most important part of the information with which the machine deals.

As in the case of the hand calculation shown in Fig. 10*a*, a machine must have components which store and process information and control the process (see Fig. 10*b*):

1. The *memory unit* plays the role of the piece of paper. In it is recorded all the required information, including the program, in the "language" of the machine. Clearly, a unit capable of performing such functions can be constructed. For example, the

memory may be a magnetic tape, on which the necessary coded information is stored, much as in an ordinary tape recorder. The memory unit of a machine is divided into *cells* which are labelled by numbers called their *addresses*. Each cell stores or is capable of storing one coded item of information; all such information, as we have already mentioned, is in numerical form.

In practical machines, the memory function may also be performed by cathode-ray tubes, magnetic drums, magnetic cores, or some combination of these devices. However, we need not distinguish between them and shall suppose for our purpose that the memory unit consists of a single piece of apparatus, say a magnetic tape.

2. The *arithmetic unit* plays the same role as a desk calculator, although the principles of its construction are quite different. It performs a given operation (for example, the addition of two numbers) by electronically converting electrical signals representing the operands into electrical signals representing the result. The input signals enter the arithmetic unit from the memory cells in which they were stored, and the output signals representing the result go to the cell in which they are to be stored. This is shown schematically in Fig. 10*b*, where the numbers in cells 11 and 12 are added and the sum stored in cell 15. In order for this operation to be performed by the machine in a given time cycle, it is necessary that connections be made at the beginning of the cycle from cells 11 and 12 to the arithmetic unit, and from the arithmetic unit to cell 15, and that the arithmetic unit be set for the proper operation (in this case, addition).

All this is to be done by the control unit.

3. The *control unit* is responsible for the functions which in Fig. 10*a* were carried out by the calculator himself. At every step of the computation it must set up the conditions for carrying out the required operation. It acts like an automatic telephone exchange, connecting those "numbers" (memory cells, input lines to the arithmetic unit, etc.) which take part in each operation. Figuratively speaking, the control block consults the program for directions and then gives the proper orders to those parts of the machine which take part in the operation to be performed.

18. MACHINE INSTRUCTIONS

Every machine is characterized by a definite set of instructions which it can execute. Every program consists of a specific combination of instructions and auxiliary numbers (parameters); these are stored in memory cells. Some machines, of which the Russian BESM is an example, have a three-address[1] format for instructions; the instruction is represented by a sequence of four numbers

$$\alpha\beta\gamma\delta,$$

of which the first indicates the operation, the next two the addresses of the two cells on whose contents the operation is to be performed, and the fourth the address of the cell in which the result is to be stored (three addresses in all).

Each instruction is written in a single cell in the form of a number whose digits are divided into four groups having the meanings indicated. For instance, in Fig. 10b, cell 1 contains the number 1 11 12 15, which is the code for the instruction "*Add* (operation 1) *the numbers in cells* 11 *and* 12 *and store the result in cell* 15." (We have divided the digits into groups of two from right to left. This convention will be used in what follows.)

Usually there are a few dozen instructions for a machine.[2] Here are some of the most common ones.

1. *Arithmetic instructions:*

(a) 1 β γ δ—Add the number in β to the number in γ and store the sum in δ.

(b) 2 β γ δ—Subtract the number in γ from the number in β and store the difference in δ.

(c) 3 β γ δ—Multiply the number in β by the number in γ and store the product in δ.

(d) 4 β γ δ—Divide the number in β by the number in γ and store the quotient in δ.

2. *Jump instructions:*

(e) 5 00 00 δ—Proceed to the instruction stored in δ (*unconditional jump*).

---

[1] Translators' Note: Most commercially manufactured machines are one-address machines. There are also two-address machines such as the MANIACs.

[2] Translators' Note: The trend is toward a larger number of instructions. Many machines now have hundreds. One (the Rice Institute machine) has about 8000.

(f) 5 01 γ δ—Proceed to the instruction stored in δ if and only if γ contains a positive number.

(g) 5 02 γ δ—Proceed to the instruction stored in δ if and only if γ contains a negative number.

3. *The "stop" order:*

0 00 00 00—Stop.

Besides the instructions listed, there are so-called *logical instructions* and others which we shall not discuss. Those given above are sufficient for constructing a wide variety of programs; we shall consider some examples in the next chapter.

Usually the instructions are executed by the machine in the order in which they occur in the memory. Deviations from this order are possible only via the execution of a jump instruction.[1]

Instructions (f) and (g) are called *conditional jumps;* they are executed only if the corresponding condition is satisfied; otherwise the machine merely skips them and goes on to the next instruction.

The operation of a machine proceeds in *cycles,* during each of which a single instruction is executed. At the beginning of each cycle the contents of the memory cell containing the instruction to be executed is brought into the control unit. The control unit then makes the necessary connections to execute the instruction. After that the next instruction is brought from the memory and executed by the control unit, etc.; this goes on until the machine is halted by a stop order.

The technical feasibility of such a control unit should not be surprising. Basically, we need no more equipment than is contained in any dial telephone exchange, where a call is automatically switched to the proper line by means of electrical signals.

We have discussed three basic components of computing machines. Actually there are other important parts, particularly those for putting the information into the machine and for transmitting the results to the machine operator, but these are not important for discussing the principles of the operation of machines or for explaining their mathematical and logical possibilities. We shall, therefore, assume in what follows that information can be put into the machine and read out of it directly via the memory unit.

[1] Translators' Note: Machines with a magnetic drum memory, such as EDSAC and the IBM 650, do not operate in this sequential fashion; instead, each instruction specifies the location of the next instruction.

6. Programs (Machine Algorithms)

In this chapter we give some examples of programs written for a three-address machine. These programs are obtained from the algorithms discussed earlier. They are analyzed to illustrate the meaning of the statement: *The operation of the machine is controlled by the program which is put into it.* That is, we show what determines the order in which the operations are performed and how solutions which often involve very long chains of operations can be controlled by a relatively small number of instructions.

The notation for machine instructions is that presented in section 18.

19. A PROGRAM FOR LINEAR EQUATIONS

Write a program to solve the system of equations

$$ax + by = c,$$
$$dx + ey = f.$$

Assume for the sake of definiteness that the coefficients a, b, c, d, e, and f are stored in consecutive memory cells, beginning with 51:

Address	Contents
51	a.
52	b
53	c
54	d
55	e
56	f

We shall also reserve cells 31–50 for storing the intermediate and final results of the computation.

The solution of the equations is

$$x = \frac{ce - fb}{ae - bd}, \quad y = \frac{af - cd}{ae - bd}.$$

To get the answer one must do six multiplications, three subtractions, and two divisions. Accordingly, our program consists of twelve instructions, stored in cells 01–12:

Address	Contents (instructions)
01	3 53 55 31
02	3 56 52 32
03	3 51 56 33
04	3 53 54 34
05	3 51 55 35
06	3 52 54 36
07	2 31 32 37
08	2 33 34 38
09	2 35 36 39
10	4 37 39 40
11	4 38 39 41
12	0 00 00 00

The instructions are brought into the control unit and carried out in succession. After the whole sequence is completed, cells 31–41 contain the following numbers:

Address	Contents
31	ce
32	fb
33	af
34	cd
35	ae
36	bd
37	$ce - fb$
38	$af - cd$
39	$ae - bd$
40	$\dfrac{ce - fb}{ae - bd}$
41	$\dfrac{af - cd}{ae - bd}$

which comprise all intermediate results of the computation, as well as the final result (cells 40 and 41).

20. ITERATION

Find the solutions of the n systems of equations

$$a_i x + b_i y = c_i,$$
$$d_i x + e_i y = f_i, \quad i = 1, 2, \ldots, n.$$

The algorithm for this problem is just an n-fold repetition of that for one system of equations of this type. Thus, it would be easy to construct an algorithm which is just a simple extension of the one of section 19, having $6n$ parameters stored in $6n$ memory cells and a total of $11n + 1$ instructions, of which the first 11 compute the solution of the first system, the second 11 the solution of the second system, etc., n times, and the $(11n + 1)$st instruction is the stop order.

However, this considerable increase in the size of the program is inefficient and can be avoided. Note that each series of 11 instructions can be obtained from the series preceding it by changing the addresses which appear in the instructions. Specifically, if the $6n$ parameters are stored in order, beginning with cell 51, then adding 6 to the first two addresses in each of the first six instructions in the program in section 19 gives an algorithm for solving the second system of equations. To keep the results apart, we must also increase the final addresses in cells 10 and 11 by 2 each time. We can thus extend the algorithm of section 19 to the more general case by means of eight *address-modification* instructions. We first place two parameters in cells 25 and 26:

Address	Contents
25	0 06 06 00
26	0 00 00 02

The eight additional instructions are:

Address	Contents
12	1 01 25 01
13	1 02 25 02
14	1 03 25 03
15	1 04 25 04
16	1 05 25 05
17	1 06 25 06
18	1 10 26 10
19	1 11 26 11

After instructions 01–19 are executed, cells 40 and 41 contain the solution to the first system of equations, as before, and cells 01–06 and 10–11 the following modified instructions:

Address	Contents
01	3 59 61 31
02	3 62 58 32
03	3 57 62 33
04	3 59 60 34
05	3 57 61 35
06	3 58 60 36
10	4 37 39 42
11	4 38 39 43

Thus, if instructions 01–19 are executed again, the second system of equations will be solved and the solution stored in addresses 42 and 43. In addition, the addresses in instructions 01–06 and 10–11 will be changed in such a way as to set things up for solving the third system of equations on the next loop, etc.

After repeating these 19 instructions as many times as we have systems of equations (and in the process, solving all the systems of equations), how do we get the machine to stop? To do this we place the parameters 0 00 00 01 and n (n is the number of systems of equations) in cells 27 and 28, respectively, and append the following three instructions to the 19 already present:

Address	Contents
20	2 28 27 28
21	5 01 28 01
22	0 00 00 00

Instruction 20 reduces the contents of cell 28 by one after each repetition of instructions 01–19. Instruction 21 is a conditional jump which transfers control to address 01 and it is carried out as long as the number in 28 is positive; each time it is executed it starts the machine off on another loop to solve the next system of equations. After n such loops, when the equations are all solved, the contents of cell 28 will be reduced to zero and the conditional jump of instruction 21 will not be carried out. The machine will then proceed to the next instruction (cell 22), which will stop the machine.

From what has been said, it is clear that the problem posed of solving n systems of equations will be solved by the program contained in cells 01–22. The structure of this program is represented in the following diagram:[1]

	Instructions		*Parameters*
01		25	0 06 06 00
02		26	0 00 00 02
03	Arithmetic	27	0 00 00 01
04		28	n
05	Operations		
06			
07			
08			
09			
10			
11			
12			
13			
14	Address		
15			
16	Modification		
17			
18			
19			
20	Loop counting		
21	Conditional jump		
22	Stop		

21. THE EUCLIDEAN ALGORITHM

We next consider a program for finding the greatest common divisor of two numbers a and b. We place the initial numbers a and b in cells 12 and 13 respectively and reserve cells 14 and 15 for the intermediate computations; when the machine stops, the final result is to appear in 15. The program is constructed from the Euclidean algorithm, given in section 1.

Address	*Contents*	*Explanation*
01	1 12 05 15	Transfer the contents of 12 to 15
02	2 12 13 14	Place the difference of 12 and 13 in 14

[1] Translators' Note: Address modification has turned out to be so important in practice that most larger machines have special devices to perform it more automatically.

48

Address	Contents	Explanation
03	5 02 14 06	Jump to 06 if the contents of 14 is negative
04	5 01 14 09	Jump to 09 if the contents of 14 is positive
05	0 00 00 00	Stop
06	1 13 05 12	Transfer the contents of 13 to 12
07	1 15 05 13	Transfer the contents of 15 to 13
08	5 00 00 01	Unconditional jump to instruction 01
09	1 13 05 12	Transfer the contents of 13 to 12
10	1 14 05 13	Transfer the contents of 14 to 13
11	5 00 00 01	Unconditional jump to instruction 01

After the first two instructions are executed we have:

Address	Contents
12	a
13	b
14	$a - b$
15	a

If $a - b = 0$ (that is, $a = b$), then the conditional transfers 03 and 04 will be passed over and instruction 05 executed, which stops the machine. Then cell 15 obviously contains the required result (compare with instruction 3 in section 1).

If $a - b < 0$ (that is, $a < b$), then instruction 03 transfers control to 06, and this and 07 interchange the locations of a and b in cells 12 and 13 (compare with instruction 4 in section 1). Then instruction 08 transfers control unconditionally to 01 again and the machine begins another loop.

If $a - b > 0$ (that is, $a > b$), then instruction 03 is ignored and instruction 04 transfers control to 09. Instructions 09 and 10 replace the numbers a and b in 12 and 13 by b and $a - b$ respectively (compare with instruction 5 in section 1). Instruction 11 then transfers control unconditionally to 01, which then begins another loop.

A sequence of loops will produce a sequence of pairs of numbers in cells 12 and 13:

$$(a_1, b_1), (a_2, b_2), \ldots, (a_i, b_i), (a_{i+1}, b_{i+1}), \ldots$$

and a sequence of numbers in cell 15:

$$a_1, a_2, \ldots, a_i, a_{i+1}, \ldots,$$

until such time as a pair of equal numbers (a_k, b_k) appears in cells 12 and 13. Instruction 05 will then stop the machine and the result a_k will be in cell 15.

49

22. OPERATION OF COMPUTING MACHINES

The preceding three examples clearly reflect the following two basic principles of the operation of automatic computing machines:

1. The instructions of the program are arranged in some pre-assigned order, which the machine generally follows in executing the program. However, the machine is capable of changing the course of the computation automatically, depending on the nature of various intermediate results. This is accomplished by introducing conditional jump instructions.

2. The machine is able to do a rather long computation using a relatively short program, because the various parts of the program can be repeated or revised automatically. This is possible since the program, being numerically coded and stored in the memory unit in the same form as any other data, may itself be modified by the machine in the course of the calculation (for example, by having the addresses in certain instructions increased or diminished).

These principles are also characteristic of the operation of the machine for problems which are not so obviously computational (arithmetic) in nature. For example, it is possible to program Theseus' algorithm (search in a labyrinth) or a known algorithm for the word problem in some associative calculus. But in order to do this, it is necessary that the machine be able to perform a few additional elementary operations and jump instructions, besides those used in the simple arithmetic problems considered above. This can be done on modern electronic machines, so that the same machine can be made to solve many types of problems simply by varying the program.

23. USES OF COMPUTING MACHINES

Not only in mathematics but in many other human activities, there are processes which can be expressed formally as a rigorously defined sequence of instructions (algorithm) and programmed for a machine. For example, in bookkeeping and economic planning, the analysis and processing of data and the compiling of balances are carried out by means of long chains of elementary operations according to fixed procedures. In other cases there are still no clear-cut, perfected algorithms, although some day such algorithms may be formulated and perfected. This is true, for example, of the problem of translation from one language into another. Given a sufficiently systematic analysis of the syntax, morphology, and word usage in a pair of languages, it would be possible to construct a satisfactory algorithm for translating, say, scientific and commercial texts from the one language into the other. (Such algorithms already exist for some pairs of languages.)

Let us consider briefly the possibility of a machine playing a game successfully. First, it is possible, in principle, to write instructions in machine language for a search for the optimum strategy according to the algorithm of section 7. In practice this will be feasible only for a game with a reasonably small tree, for example, games like the match games of sections 4 and 5 for which the number of matches is fairly small. Secondly, if one already knows an optimum strategy for a game, he can program it for a machine. In the case of complicated games for which no strategies are known or for which the known strategies are too cumbersome to be handled, one is forced to confine himself to methods based on only a partial analysis of the game, methods forming the so-called *tactics* of the game. For example, in chess it is possible to set up a system of values for the pieces, in which the king is assigned a very large number of points, the queen a smaller number, the rooks a still smaller number, and so on, with the pawns having the smallest value. In addition, we evaluate the advantages of the positions (mobility, control of the center of the board, protection of the king, etc.). The difference between the sum of the points for white and black characterizes the material and positional advantage of white at each step of the game. The simplest algorithm consists in listing all possible moves for a given position and then selecting the one which gives the greatest advantage from the point of view of the established system of values. A better, but more complicated, algorithm consists in examining all possible combinations of three or four consecutive moves and selecting the optimum move on this basis.

From what we have said, it becomes clearer how many kinds of intellectual tasks can be performed according to a definite algorithm. In all these cases it is possible, in principle, to program the operations for a machine with automatic control. In particular, programs for translating languages and playing chess have been written and run successfully on machines (see reference [5]).

7. The Need for a More Precise Definition of "Algorithm"

24. THE EXISTENCE OF ALGORITHMS

Our previous discussion shows the strong connection which exists between algorithms and automatic computing machines. Obviously, any process which can be performed by a machine can be written as an algorithm. Conversely, all algorithms which have so far been constructed, as well as those which may be expected in the present state of science, can in principle be performed by machine.

The last statement requires some clarification. As we have already seen, the actual application of an algorithm may turn out to be very lengthy, and the job of recording all of the information involved may be enormous. On the other hand, the memory units of machines have a limited capacity (since the number of memory cells is finite and the capacity of each cell is limited). Therefore, it may turn out to be impossible to execute an algorithm under existing conditions.

This can be illustrated by the Euclidean algorithm. The very simple problem of finding the greatest common divisor of two numbers cannot be solved by hand if it requires more paper and ink than is available. Similarly, a problem will not be solvable by machine if it requires more memory space than there is in the machine.

In such cases we say that an algorithm is *potentially realizable* if it leads to the required result in a finite number of steps (even though this number may be very large). In other words, it would be possible to use the algorithm in a machine which had an unlimited memory capacity.

The connection between the idea of an algorithm and the idea of an automatic machine with a memory of infinite capacity leads to a clearer understanding of the nature of each. However, for all of our emphasis on their connection, we still have not defined either of these ideas precisely. An exact mathematical definition of the notion of algorithms (and, at the same time, of automatic computing machines) was not produced until the 1930's. Why, through the course of many centuries, have mathematicians tolerated without any particular qualms an unclear notion of algorithms? Why is it that only recently has an acute need for a definition sufficiently exact for mathematical discussion arisen?

Earlier, the term "algorithm" occurred in mathematics only in connection with concrete algorithms, where *an assertion of the existence of an algorithm was always accompanied by a description of such an algorithm.* Under these conditions it was necessary to show only that the system of formal instructions when applied to any data in fact led automatically to the desired result. Thus, the need for a precise definition of the notion of algorithm never arose, although every mathematician had a working idea of what the term meant. However, in the course of mathematical progress, facts began to accumulate which radically changed this situation. The motive force was the natural desire of mathematicians to construct increasingly powerful algorithms for solving increasingly general types of problems.

Recall the algorithm for finding square roots. We might wish to generalize this problem: to construct an algorithm for finding the root of any degree of any given number. It is natural to expect that such an algorithm will be more difficult to construct, but the prospect of having it is attractive. We may go even further. Finding the nth root of a number a means solving the equation

$$x^n - a = 0$$

(finding the roots of the equation). We can formulate the still more general problem:

Construct an algorithm for finding all roots of any equation of the form

$$a_n x^n + a_{n-1} x^{n-1} + \cdots + a_1 x + a_0 = 0, \qquad (*)$$

where n is an arbitrary positive integer.[1]

The construction of such an algorithm is still more difficult. In fact, the basic content of the theory of equations amounts to the construction of just this algorithm; it is of the greatest importance.

---

[1] More precisely, for any integer k, find a decimal approximation to the roots which is correct to within $\dfrac{1}{10^k}$.

25. THE DEDUCIBILITY PROBLEM

The examples given show the natural striving of mathematicians to find increasingly powerful algorithms to solve increasingly general types of problems. Of course, the example of solving all equations of the form (*) does not represent the limit to which one might go. If we want to push this desire for increasingly general algorithms to the extreme, we must inevitably consider this problem:

Construct an algorithm for solving any mathematical problem.

This is a problem so general that it might be considered an insolent challenge to mathematics as a whole. Besides this, it can be criticized on the grounds that it is not clear what is meant by "any mathematical problem." At the same time, the great allure of solving such a problem cannot be doubted.

This problem has its own history. The great German mathematician and philosopher Leibniz (1646–1716) dreamed of an all-inclusive method for solving any problem. Although he was unable to find it, Leibniz still thought that the time would come when it would be discovered, and that any argument among mathematicians could then automatically be settled with pencil and paper.

Later, the problem received some refinement in the form of one of the most famous problems of mathematical logic, the *deducibility problem*. Since we do not have room for a complete treatment of the problem, we shall merely sketch its general outlines.

As is well known, the axiomatic method in mathematics consists in deriving all theorems in a given theory by formal logical steps from certain axioms which are accepted without proof. The first of all axiomatic theories was geometry, but in modern mathematics almost all theories are constructed axiomatically. Mathematical logic employs a special "language of formulas" that enables us to write any proposition of a mathematical theory as a uniquely determined formula.

In the terminology which we used earlier for an associative calculus (section 11), we may say that such a formula is a word in a special alphabet containing symbols to denote logical operations such as negation, conjunction, and implication, as well as the usual mathematical symbols, such as parentheses, and letters to denote functions and variables. However, the chief similarity to an associative calculus consists in the possibility of writing the logical derivation of a statement S from a premise R in the form of formal transformations of words, very similar to the admissible substitutions in an associative calculus. This allows us to speak of a *logical calculus,* with a system of admissible transformations representing elementary acts of logical deduction, from which any logical inference, of arbitrary complexity, may be built. An example of such an admissible transformation is the elimination of two consecutive negations in a formula; thus, "not unproved" may be transformed into "proved" (compare this with the admissible substitution $aa - \wedge$ in Example 2 of section 14).

The question of the logical deducibility of the proposition S from the premise R in a logical calculus becomes the question of the existence of a deductive chain leading from the word representing R to the word representing S. The deducibility problem may now be formulated as follows:

For any two words (formulas) R and S in a logical calculus, determine whether or not there exists a deductive chain from R to S.

The solution is supposed to be an algorithm for solving any problem of this type (any R and S). Such an algorithm would give a general method for solving problems in all mathematical theories which are constructed axiomatically (or rather, in all *finitely axiomatizable* theories). The validity of any statement S in such a theory merely means that it can be deduced from the system of axioms, or what is the same thing, that it can be deduced from the statement R which asserts that all the axioms hold. Then the application of the algorithm would determine whether or not the proposition S were valid. Moreover, if the proposition S were valid, then we could find a corresponding deductive chain in the logical calculus and from this recover a chain of inference which would prove the proposition. The proposed algorithm would in fact be a single effective method for solving almost all of the mathematical problems which have been formulated and remain unsolved to this day. That is why constructing such an "all-inclusive algorithm" and an "omnipotent machine" to match it is so appealing a prospect and at the same time so difficult.

Despite the long and persistent efforts of many great men, the difficulties of finding such an algorithm have remained insurmountable. Furthermore, similar difficulties were soon encountered in trying to find algorithms for certain problems of a far less general nature. Among these were Hilbert's problem on Diophantine equations (section 3), as well as others which will be discussed below.

As a result of many fruitless attempts to construct such algorithms, it became clear that the difficulties involved are basic, and it came to be suspected that *it is not possible to construct an algorithm for every class of problems.*

The assertion that a certain class of problems cannot be solved algorithmically is not simply a statement that no algorithm has yet been discovered. It is the statement that such an algorithm in fact can *never* be discovered, in other words, that no such algorithm can exist. This assertion must be based on some sort of mathematical proof; however, such a proof makes no sense until we have a precise definition of "algorithm," since until then it is not clear what it is we are trying to prove impossible. It is useful to remember at this point that in the history of mathematics there have been other problems for which solutions had been sought in vain for a long time, and for which it was only later proved that solutions could not be obtained. Examples are the problem of trisecting the angle and the problem of solving the general fifth degree equation by radicals.

A method of bisecting an angle using compass and straightedge is known to every schoolboy. The ancient Greeks tried to solve the problem of trisecting an angle using compass and straightedge. It was later proved that trisection of an arbitrary angle by such means is impossible. It is also well known that the solution of a quadratic equation can be written in terms of the coefficients by means of a formula which employs the signs for the arithmetic operations and the radical sign. There are also formulas in radicals, which are extremely complicated, for third and fourth degree equations. A search for similar solutions by radicals for equations of degree higher than four was carried on unsuccessfully until the beginning of the nineteenth century, when the following remarkable result was finally established.

For any n greater than or equal to 5, it is impossible to express the roots of the general nth degree equation in terms of its coefficients by means of the arithmetic operations and the operation of extracting roots.

In both these cases the proof of impossibility turned out to be feasible only after there were precise definitions to answer the questions "What is meant by a compass and straightedge construction?" and "What is meant by solving an equation in radicals?" Note that these two definitions gave a more precise meaning to certain special algorithms, namely, the algorithm for solving an equation in radicals (not for the solution of equations in general) and the algorithm for trisecting an angle with compass and straightedge (not for trisecting by arbitrary devices).

26. FORMULATION OF A DEFINITION OF "ALGORITHM"

Until recently, there was no precise definition of the concept "algorithm," and therefore the construction of such a definition came to be one of the major problems of modern mathematics. It is very important to point out that the formulation of a definition of "algorithm" (or of any other mathematical definition) must be considered as not merely an arbitrary agreement among mathematicians as to what the meaning of the word "algorithm" should be. The definition has to reflect accurately the substance of those ideas which are actually held, however vaguely, and which have already been illustrated by many examples. With this aim, a series of investigations was undertaken beginning in the 1930's for characterizing all the methods which were actually used in constructing algorithms. The problem was to formulate a definition of the concept of *algorithm* which would be complete not only in form but, more important, in substance. Various workers proceeded from different logical starting points, and because of this, several definitions were proposed. However, it turned out that all of these were equivalent, and that they defined the same concept; this was the modern definition of *algorithm*. The fact that all of these apparently different definitions were really essentially the same is quite significant; it indicates that we have a worthwhile definition.

From the point of view of machine mathematics, we are especially interested in *the form of the definition which proceeds from a consideration of the processes performable by machines.* For such a rigorous mathematical definition it is necessary to represent the operation of the machine in the form of some standard scheme, which has as simple a logical structure as possible, but which is sufficiently precise for use in mathematical investigations. This was first done by the English mathematician Turing, who proposed a very general but very simple conception of a computing machine. It should be noted that the Turing machine was first described in 1937,[1] that is, before the construction of modern computing machines. Turing proceeded simply on the general idea of equating the operation of a machine to the work of a human calculator who is following definite instructions. Our presentation of his ideas will utilize the general ideas of electronic machines now in use.

---

[1] See [1] in the Bibliography, p. 101.

8. The Turing Machine

The distinguishing features of the Turing machine, as compared with the electronic machines described in Chapters 5 and 6, are the following.

1. In the Turing machine the reduction of a process to elementary operations is carried, in a certain sense, to its limit. Thus, for example, the operation of addition, which in the electronic machine is considered as a single operation, is broken down further into a chain of simpler operations. This, of course, considerably increases the number of steps in calculations by the machine, but at the same time greatly simplifies the logical structure, a great convenience for theoretical investigations.

2. In the Turing machine the memory unit[1] is conceived of as a tape, infinitely long in both directions and divided into cells. Of course, no real machine can have an infinite memory, and the Turing machine is in this sense an idealization which reflects the possibility of increasing the memory capacity of any machine. This idealization was justified earlier (section 24) in our discussion of the connection between automatic machines and the concept of a potentially realizable algorithm.

27. DEFINITION OF TURING MACHINES

We now move on to a detailed definition of a Turing machine.
1. There is a finite set of symbols

$$s_1, s_2, \ldots, s_k,$$

the so-called *external alphabet,* in which is coded the information fed into the machine, as well as the information which the machine produces. For the sake of generality, it is convenient to assume that among the symbols of the external alphabet is an *empty letter*, say, s_1. Putting the empty letter into a memory cell erases the symbol which previously appeared there, and we say that a cell containing the empty letter is an empty cell.

---

[1] Specifically, the so-called external memory.

Each cell can contain at most one symbol. Each piece of information is represented by a finite string of symbols of the external alphabet, not including the empty letter, and is stored in consecutive cells on the tape. The initial information is introduced onto the tape. The machine then begins to operate, and in the course of each of its cycles the initial information is transformed into intermediate information. At the end of each cycle, all the information on the tape makes up the intermediate information at that stage. The initial information can be any finite system of symbols in the external alphabet (any word in this alphabet) distributed among the memory cells in any fashion. However, depending on what initial information $\mathfrak{A}$ was given, there are two possible cases.

(a) After a finite number of cycles the machine halts, having received a stop order, and there appears on the tape the representation of some information $\mathfrak{B}$. In this case we say that the machine is *applicable* to the initial information $\mathfrak{A}$ and that it has transformed it into the resulting information $\mathfrak{B}$.

(b) A stop order is never received, and the machine never halts. In this case we say that the machine is *inapplicable* to the initial information $\mathfrak{A}$.

We say that *a machine can solve a given class of problems* if it is applicable to the information representing (in a fixed code) any problem of the class and if it transforms this information into information representing the solution (in the same code).

2. Instead of the three-address instruction format of the machine of chapters 5 and 6, the Turing machine (like some actual computers) uses a one-address format; that is, only one memory cell figures in any step of a computation. (We call the single memory cell involved in a given Turing machine instruction the *scanned cell* of that step.) For instance, the three-address instruction for adding the numbers in β and γ and storing the result in δ might be replaced by the sequence of three instructions:

(a) Transmit the contents of β to the adder.
(b) Transmit the contents of γ to the adder.
(c) Transmit the contents of the adder to δ.

In the Turing machine the system of elementary operations and the system of one-address instructions is simplified even further. In each cycle the instruction changes the symbol s_i contained in the scanned cell into some other symbol s_j. If $i = j$, then the symbol in the scanned cell is not altered; if $j = 1$, then the symbol in the scanned cell is simply erased. Further, in going from one cycle of the machine to the next, the address of the scanned cell cannot change by more than 1. That is, the next cell to be scanned is either one space to the right, one space to the left, or the same cell.

If the contents of a particular cell are needed in the calculation, the machine searches for this cell by examining all of the cells one by one until it finds the right one. This greatly lengthens the process, but it also affords the following convenience: in the instructions of the program, instead of an arbitrary address for the scanned cell, we can limit ourselves to three standard addresses, which are represented by special symbols:

R—scan the next cell to the right,
L—scan the next cell to the left,
S—scan the same cell again.

3. For processing the numerical information contained in the memory unit, the electronic machine described in Chapters 5 and 6 has an arithmetic unit, which may be in any one of a finite number of states: the addition state, the subtraction state, etc. To carry out any operation in the arithmetic unit, paths must be established for transmitting not only the numbers on which the operation is to be performed but also the signals which set the unit for the proper operation. This is illustrated in Fig. 10b. In the Turing machine, the processing of information is performed by a *logical unit* $\mathcal{L}$, which also can be in any of a finite number of states. Let

$$q_1, q_2, \ldots, q_m$$

be special symbols introduced to denote these states. The unit has two input lines: through one of them comes the symbol s_i on the square being scanned, and through the other comes the symbol q_l of the state which the unit is in during the current cycle. Then the unit transmits a "transformed" sign s_j, which is uniquely determined by the two inputs s_i and q_l, into the cell being scanned via its output line. The instructions which specify what the machine is to do on each cycle are of one of the forms:

$$Rq_l, \; Lq_l, \; Sq_l \quad (l = 1, 2, \ldots, m),$$

where the first symbol specifies the address of the square to be scanned (see above) and the second puts the logical unit into its proper state. The symbols R, L, S, q_1, $q_2, \ldots, q_m$ form the *internal alphabet* of the machine.

In addition to the output s_j, the logical unit determines what instruction is to be put into the control unit to begin the next cycle. Thus, the logical unit must have not only one output line for the symbol s_j to be copied onto the tape, but also two output lines which transmit the two symbols of the next instruction to the control unit (see Fig. 11). It is essential that the *output triple* s_j, P, q_i depend only on the *input pair* of symbols s_i, q_n of the current cycle.[1] This means that the logical unit is like a function which associates a triple of symbols s_j, P, q_l with every pair of symbols s_i, q_n. (In all, there are $k \cdot m$ such pairs.) It is convenient to represent this function (called the *logical function* of the machine) as a rectangular table with one column for each state symbol and one row for each symbol of the external alphabet and having the output triple at the intersection of the row and column of the input pair. We shall call this table the *functional matrix* of the machine; an example of such a matrix is illustrated in Fig. 12.[2]

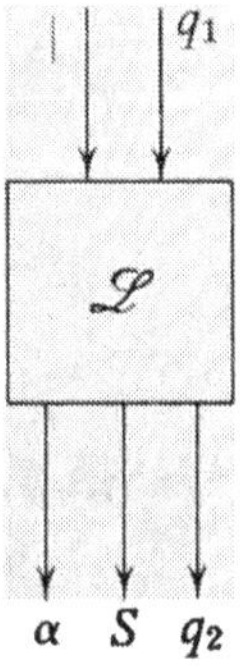

Fig. 11

	q_1	q_2	q_3	q_4	q_5
$\wedge$	$\wedge R q_4$	$\wedge L q_3$	$\wedge R q_1$	$\wedge S q_5$	$\wedge S q_5$
$\vert$	$\alpha S q_2$	$\beta S q_1$	$\vert R q_1$	$\vert L q_1$	$\vert S q_5$
α	$\alpha L q_1$	$\alpha R q_2$	$\vert L q_3$	$\wedge R q_4$	$\alpha S q_5$
β	$\beta L q_1$	$\beta R q_2$	$\wedge L q_3$	$\vert R q_4$	$\beta S q_5$

Fig. 12

28. THE OPERATION OF TURING MACHINES

It is clear that the operation of a Turing machine is completely determined by its functional matrix, so that two Turing machines with the same matrix are indistinguishable as regards what they do.

[1] P can be any of the symbols R, L, S.

[2] Let us suppose for the moment that the external alphabet consists of the symbols $\wedge$, $\vert$, α, β, where $\wedge$ represents the empty letter.

The structure of a machine and the function and interaction of its various parts can be seen from the general *structural diagram* for Turing machines (Fig. 13).

This diagram reflects the division of the memory into inner and outer. The outer memory is represented by the cells on the infinite tape in which information coded in the symbols of the outer alphabet is to be stored. The inner memory consists of two cells for storage of the next instruction: the state symbol is stored in the Q-cell and the tape motion symbol in the P-cell. The symbols P, q_l put out

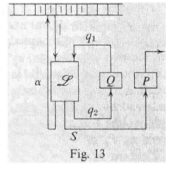

Fig. 13

by the logical unit at the beginning of a cycle are stored in these two cells until the beginning of the next cycle, when they are transmitted to the control unit. The function of the control unit can be reduced to that of moving the tape one space (or not at all) in the direction specified by the P-symbol. The state sign could be transmitted directly from the Q-cell into $\mathscr{L}$, forming a so-called feedback line, by which the symbol put out by $\mathscr{L}$ on the preceding cycle is fed back into $\mathscr{L}$.

The operation of the Turing machine is as follows. Before it starts, the initial information is put onto the tape and a specific cell (in Fig. 13, the cell containing the fourth stroke from the right) is moved into the "scanning position," and the symbols of the initial state and initial direction of tape motion (say, q_1 and S) are put into the Q and P-cells. From this point on the machine operates automatically in the unique fashion defined by its functional matrix. Observe, for example, what happens in the case of the functional matrix of Fig. 12.

First cycle. $(|, q_1) \rightarrow \alpha S q_2$: the stroke is replaced by α, the tape does not move, and the machine changes to state q_2.

Second cycle. $(\alpha, q_2) \rightarrow \alpha R q_2$: the α remains unchanged, the next cell to the right moves into the scanning position, and the machine stays in state q_2.

Third cycle. $(|, q_2) \rightarrow \beta S q_1$: the stroke is replaced by β, the tape does not move, and the machine changes to state q_1.

And so forth.

62

As may be seen from the last column of Fig. 12, the machine will stop only if the state q_5 is produced at some stage of the process. If this happens, the scanned symbol will not be changed, and the machine will keep scanning the same cell and remain in the same state (q_5). This constitutes a *stop-condition,* signaling the end of the calculation.

The operation of a Turing machine can also be carried out by hand. To do this it is convenient to use the notion of *configuration.* By the *k*th *configuration* we mean a diagram of the tape at the beginning of the *k*th cycle, with the symbol representing the state of the logical unit during this cycle written below the scanned cell. In this way we clearly indicate the input pair of symbols in this cycle, and by referring to the functional matrix, we obtain the output triple, which then defines the $(k + 1)$st configuration.

In the above example, the first and second configurations are:

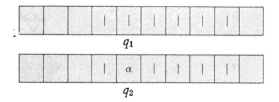

with input pairs $|q_1$ and αq_2, respectively. The transfer from the first configuration to the second is carried out by the output triple $\alpha S q_2$ corresponding to the input pair $|q_1$ in Fig. 12.

From now on we shall write the functional matrix in a simpler and more convenient form. Instead of always writing the output triple $s_j P q_l$ in full, we shall omit the symbol s_j or q_l if it is the same as the corresponding input symbol and shall not mark the zero tape-motion S. We may then have completely empty columns, corresponding to a stop-condition. Such columns may then be omitted from the matrix, as in Fig. 14, which shows the functional matrix of Fig. 12 in this simplified notation, with "!" representing the stop-condition. (Henceforth, we shall always use "!" to represent the stop-condition.)

	q_1	q_2	q_3	q_4
$\wedge$	$R q_4$	$L q_3$	$R q_1$	!
$|$	αq_2	βq_1	$R q_1$	$L q_1$
α	L	R	$| L$	$\wedge R$
β	L	R	$\wedge L$	$| R$

Fig. 14

63

It is easier to see from Fig. 14 than from Fig. 12 that if the machine scans the symbol α in the state q_1, it will begin a series of moves to the left, passing over all occurrences of α or β without changing them and remaining in the state q_1, until it encounters a stroke or an empty cell. Only then will the machine go into a different state.

In the next chapter we shall discuss the construction of Turing machines which carry out certain simple numerical algorithms. (In accordance with the preceding section, by the construction of a Turing machine we shall mean simply the construction of the corresponding functional matrix, which thus constitutes a standard form for the algorithm.) We shall also discuss some more general matters concerning the construction of Turing machines (functional matrices).

9. The Realization of Algorithms in Turing Machines

29. TRANSFORMING n INTO $n + 1$ IN DECIMAL NOTATION

The following problem is to be solved:

Given a positive integer n written in decimal form, find the decimal representation of the number n + 1.

Take for the external alphabet the empty symbol $\wedge$ and the ten digits 0, 1, 2, 3, 4, 5, 6, 7, 8, 9. The machine may be in one of two states: q_0 (the operating state) and ! (stopped). The given number n, as well as the resulting number $n + 1$, is written in the decimal system by means of a series of digits in consecutive cells (one digit per cell). The functional matrix is given in Fig. 15, if we ignore the last column and last row (whose significance will be explained shortly). At the outset, the machine is set to scan the rightmost digit of the number n (that is, the digit in the units' place) and is in state q_0. If this digit is less than 9, the machine replaces the digit by the next higher digit and stops, as shown in the functional matrix. If the digit is 9, then the machine changes it to a zero and moves one space to the left, while remaining in the state q_0 (this provides for carrying a 1 to the next digit). If the number ends with k nines, the machine will stop after $k + 1$ cycles.

	q_0	q_1
0	1 !	
1	2 !	
2	3 !	
3	4 !	
4	5 !	
5	6 !	
6	7 !	
7	8 !	
8	9 !	
9	0 L	
$\wedge$	1 !	
		L	$\wedge L q_0$

Fig. 15

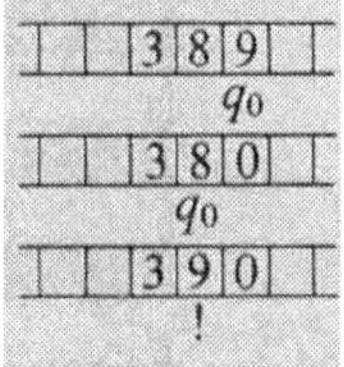

		3	8	9		

q_0

		3	8	0		

q_0

		3	9	0		

!

Fig. 16

Fig. 16 shows the configurations for $n = 389$.

We shall now explain the meaning of the extended table of Fig. 15. This is a functional matrix which has one extra state q_1 and one additional symbol | in the external alphabet. If the machine is initially in the state q_0 and the symbol | appears nowhere on the tape, then the operation of the machine will proceed exactly as in the last example. This is clear from the fact that under those conditions the last row and last column of the table will play no role.

But the machine can do other things besides solve the problems considered above. Suppose that the tape contains the decimal representation of some number n and also several strokes immediately to the right of n. Consider the operation of the machine with this functional matrix if initially the machine is set to scan the rightmost stroke and is in state q_1. In the first cycle (input pair $|q_1$), the stroke is erased and the machine shifts one space to the left and shifts into state q_0 (output triple $\wedge Lq_0$). The machine then keeps shifting left (leaving the other strokes as they are and remaining in state q_0) until it comes to the rightmost digit of n. From this point on, the machine simply carries out the preceding algorithm; that is, it transforms the number n into the number $n + 1$ and stops when this is done.

In short, the machine reduces the number of strokes by one and changes n into $n + 1$. We call this process a *controlled transition* from the decimal representation of n to the decimal representation of $n + 1$. Fig. 17 shows the configurations for five strokes and $n = 389$.

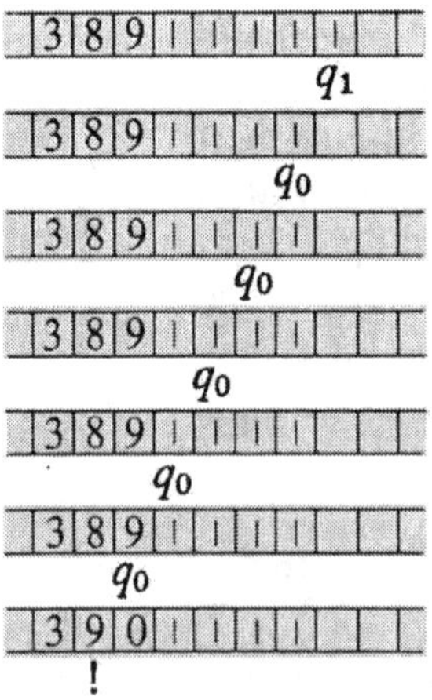

	q_0	q_1	q_2
0	1 q_2	!	R
1	2 q_2	!	R
2	3 q_2	!	R
3	4 q_2	!	R
4	5 q_2	!	R
5	6 q_2	!	R
6	7 q_2	!	R
7	8 q_2	!	R
8	9 q_2	!	R
9	0 L	!	R
$\wedge$	1 q_2	!	Lq_1
$|$	L	$\wedge Lq_0$	R

Fig. 17

Fig. 18

30. CONVERSION INTO DECIMAL NOTATION

We shall construct the functional matrix for a machine (an algorithm) to solve the following class of problems. *Given a finite set of strokes written in consecutive cells* (such a collection of strokes will be called a *string of strokes*), *write the number of strokes in decimal form.* In short, count the strokes.

Such a matrix is given in Fig. 18. To convince oneself that this table actually represents the required machine (algorithm), it is helpful to compare it with Fig. 15. The q_0 column in Fig. 18 is the same as the corresponding column in Fig. 15, with a new state q_2 substituted for "!". The difference in the q_1 column has no bearing on the operation of the matrix of Fig. 15. Therefore, if the tape contains the decimal representation of a number n, followed by a string of strokes and the initial conditions are the same as in the last example (that is, the machine is in state q_1 and scans the rightmost stroke), then the machine will begin by executing the same process as that of Fig. 15; that is, it will erase the rightmost stroke and change n into $n + 1$. However, the machine of Fig. 15 would then go into the state ! and the process would terminate, whereas the machine of Fig. 18 enters state q_2 and the process continues. In particular, if the initial configuration is that of Fig. 17, then configuration 8 will be that shown in Fig. 19. From the q_2-column

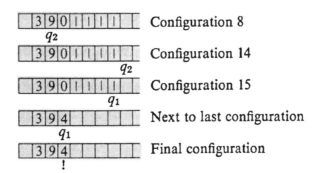

Fig. 19

of Fig. 18 we can see how the process proceeds: the machine begins to shift to the right, skipping all digits and strokes, until it comes to an empty cell (configuration 14, Fig. 19). The input pair

$\wedge q_2$ causes it to go into state q_1 and shift to the left (configuration 15, Fig. 19). The machine now is scanning the rightmost stroke and is in state q_1. This sets the initial conditions for another loop analogous to the first. In the second loop, another stroke will be erased and the number $n + 1$ changed into $n + 2$. If there are k strokes to start with, then after k loops all of the strokes will have been erased and the number n replaced by $n + k$. At the end of the kth loop the machine will be in state q_1 again and the scanned cell will contain not a stroke (for they have all been erased) but the right-most digit of the number $n + k$ (next to last configuration of Fig. 19). Referring to Fig. 18, we see that this stops the machine (final configuration, Fig. 19).

From what we have said it follows that if the tape initially contains the digit 0 and a string of k strokes, then the machine will erase all of the strokes and change the 0 to the decimal representation of k (the number of strokes). But the same is true if we start with no digits at all, but merely the string of strokes, since in states q_0 and q_1 the machine treats an empty cell the same way as it does the digit 0 (see Fig. 18). Therefore, the table given in Fig. 18 in fact represents an algorithm which gives the decimal representation of the number of strokes in any string.

PROBLEM. Construct a functional matrix for a machine (algorithm) analogous to that of section 29 for transforming the decimal representation of any number n into the decimal representation of $n - 1$ (for $n \geq 1$). Also, construct a functional matrix for a machine analogous to that of section 30 for converting the decimal representation of any number n into a string of n strokes.

31. ADDITION

We next consider some examples of Turing machines for solving arithmetic problems. In these problems the initial data and the results will be positive integers. We agree to represent any positive integer by a string of that number of strokes. If several numbers enter into a problem, we shall separate the strings of strokes representing them by a special symbol, say an asterisk, *, which we shall include in the external alphabet.

A pair of numbers is put on the tape, for example:

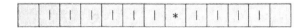

We must find their sum, which in this case is:

Note that the machine cannot simply remove the asterisk, since in that case there
would be an empty cell between the strokes
and the remaining strokes would not form a
string. Fig. 20 shows the functional matrix
of a machine which will add the two numbers.

Initial conditions: The machine is in state
q_0 and scans the leftmost stroke (configuration 1 of Fig. 21).

	q_0	q_1	q_2
I	$\wedge R q_2$	L	R
$\wedge$	R	$R q_0$	$I q_1$
*	$\wedge$!	L	R

Fig. 20

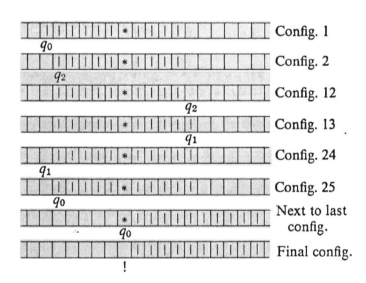

Fig. 21

First cycle: The machine erases the scanned stroke, shifts to the
right, and goes into state q_2 (configuration 2).

The following cycles are right shifts, skipping all the strokes and
the asterisk (see the q_2-column), until the machine scans an empty

cell (configuration 12). Then (input pair $\wedge q_2$) the machine marks a stroke in the empty cell and goes into state q_1 (configuration 13). The machine shifts to the left, skipping all the strokes and the asterisk, until it scans an empty cell again (configuration 24). It then (input pair $\wedge q_1$) shifts to the right to scan the leftmost stroke and goes into state q_0 (configuration 25). As a result of this loop the leftmost stroke has been moved to the right-hand end of the string, which is to the right of the asterisk. If there are initially k strokes to the left of the asterisk, then after k loops all of them will have been moved to the right of the asterisk. At the end of the last loop, the machine will be scanning not a stroke, since there are none left, but rather the asterisk and will be in state q_0 (next to last configuration). The next cycle (input pair $*q_0$) will erase the asterisk and stop the machine (final configuration). We then have the required sum on the tape.

32. REPEATED SUMMATION AND MULTIPLICATION

We want to modify the table of Fig. 20 so that, given a pair of numbers n and m on the tape, for instance:

the machine will begin an infinite process which consists of the following: the addition of the number m which is to the left of the asterisk to the number n which is to the right, followed by the addition of m to the resulting sum $n + m$, followed by the addition of m to the sum $n + 2m$, and so on, without end. For this the number on the left must not be erased during an addition, since it must be available for the next addition. This can be done by replacing the strokes on the left by some other symbols instead of erasing them. Fig. 22 shows a functional matrix in which the letter α performs this function. The empty symbol in the first row of Fig. 20 is replaced by α in the first row of Fig. 22, and the first three spaces in the newly added α-row of Fig. 22 are the same as the $\wedge$-row of Fig. 20. Further, so that the machine will not be stopped after the first addition, the stop-condition of

	q_0	q_1	q_2	q_3
I	$\alpha R q_2$	L	R	
$\wedge$	R	$R q_0$	I $q_1 R$	q_0
$*$	q_3	L	R	L
α	R	$R q_0$	I q_1	L

Fig. 22

70

Fig. 20 must be replaced by the symbol for some other state, which will serve to continue the process, and which we shall call q_3. For this new symbol there must be an additional column in the table.

There is no stop-condition in Fig. 22, and therefore the process which the table describes cannot be finite. The reader can now easily convince himself that the corresponding machine will perform an unending series of additions of the left-hand number to the right-hand number. If initially there are no strokes to the right of the asterisk, that is, if the right-hand number is zero, then the machine will produce m strokes to the right, then $2m$, then $3m$, and so on, without end.

PROBLEM. Construct a functional matrix for multiplication.

Hint. Use the previous table as a basis, and modify it so that the process of repeated summation does not continue indefinitely, but stops after a number of loops equal to the multiplier (after each loop, erase one stroke from a set representing the multiplier).

33. THE EUCLIDEAN ALGORITHM

We now consider a Turing machine for the Euclidean algorithm (finding the greatest common divisor of two numbers a and b). We have already described this algorithm twice—first by means of verbal instructions (section 1) and secondly in the form of a program for an automatic computing machine (section 21). This time we shall present it as the functional matrix of a Turing machine and shall examine the process of calculation in the machine. This process is composed of alternating *comparison loops* and *subtraction loops*, corresponding to the *elementary operations of comparison and subtraction* in an electronic machine. The functional matrix is that shown in Fig. 14; its external alphabet consists of four symbols:

$$\wedge, |, \alpha, \beta.$$

The numbers will be represented by strings of strokes, as before. In order to avoid details which are not essential and only serve to complicate matters, we shall agree to put the two sets of strokes representing the given numbers onto the tape consecutively, with no gap or separation by an asterisk; initially the machine will scan the rightmost stroke of the left-hand number. After the detailed analysis given below, the reader as an exercise should be able to change the given functional matrix to handle other initial conditions (for example, if the strings of strokes are separated by an asterisk and the machine is initially scanning an arbitrary cell). Note that the letters α and β play the role of temporary markers to aid in "remembering" certain situations which arise in the course of the computation.

We shall use configurations to describe the application of the algorithm to the simple case of $a = 4$, $b = 6$. The first configuration has the following appearance:

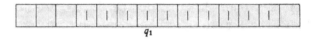

q_1

Only states q_1 and q_2 take part in the comparison loops and only q_3 and q_4 in the subtraction loops.

The machine first examines the numbers on the tape to determine which is larger. It works in much the same way as might a human calculator who had to compare the number of units in two long sequences, that is, by checking off a unit from each sequence in turn, until one of them is exhausted. Thus, the machine changes one stroke of the first number to an α, then changes one stroke of the second number to a β; then it returns to the first number and changes one of its strokes to an α, etc.

In the first four cycles, the machine produces the configurations shown in Fig. 23. At the end of the fourth cycle, the machine has "crossed out" one stroke in each number and is about to begin to shift to the left in search for the next stroke in the left-hand number. After several additional cycles, configuration I of Fig. 24 appears on the tape; the first number is exhausted, but the second is not. The search for a

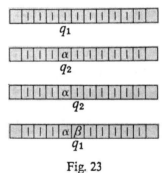

Fig. 23

stroke to the left is unsuccessful and leads to configuration II; the comparison loop has now been completed, using only states q_1 and q_2. The next cycle gives configuration III.

As shown in the q_4-column of Fig. 14, the machine now begins to shift to the right, changing all α's into empty symbols (in other words, erasing them) and all β's into strokes. After the last β has

72

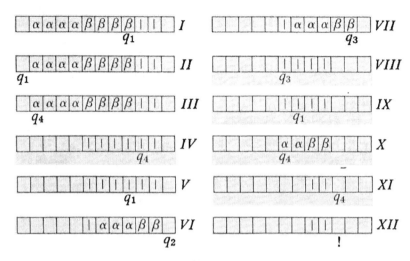

Fig. 24

been replaced by a stroke, the tape shows configuration *IV*, and after the next cycle, configuration *V*. In this way, after a comparison loop and a subtraction loop, the smaller number a has been erased, and the larger number b has been split into a and $b - a$; the machine is scanning the rightmost stroke of the left-hand number and is in state q_1. This means that the comparison cycle will be repeated, but now on the numbers a and $b - a$, instead of a and b. As we already know, this is simply the basis of the Euclidean algorithm.

We now start another comparison loop. But this time it ends by exhausting the right-hand number, which turns out to be smaller. Three strokes of the left-hand number have been changed to α's, both strokes of the right-hand number have been changed to β's, and the machine has come to an empty cell (configuration *VI*).

The next cycle gives configuration *VII*, which begins another subtraction loop. The machine shifts to the left, erasing all β's and changing all α's to strokes; after the last of these changes we have configuration *VIII*, followed by configuration *IX*. This ends the subtraction loop and begins the following comparison loop. The process continues until the problem reduces to the case of two equal numbers (in our example, we are already at that point). Then comes the last comparison loop, which must lead to the final answer. This gives configuration *X*, the last subtraction gives configuration *XI*, and we finally arrive at the result *XII*.

When constructing new functional matrices it is convenient, when possible, to use matrices previously constructed. This can be done whenever the new algorithm considered is, in a certain sense, a combination of previously constructed algorithms. We can clarify this by an example. Suppose that we are required to construct the functional matrix for an algorithm which will change a given pair of numbers, represented by strings of strokes, into their greatest common divisor, written in decimal form. Since this algorithm can be obtained as the result of the *composition* (that is, consecutive application) of two earlier algorithms—first that of section 33, then that of section 30—its functional matrix, shown in Fig. 25, can be

	q_1	q_2	q_3	q_4	p_0	p_1	p_2
0					$1p_2$	!	R
1					$2p_2$	!	R
2					$3p_2$	!	R
3					$4p_2$	!	R
4					$5p_2$	!	R
5					$6p_2$	!	R
6					$7p_2$	!	R
7					$8p_2$	!	R
8					$9p_2$	!	R
9					$0L$	!	R
∧	Rq_4	Lq_3	Rq_1	p_2	$1p_2$	!	Lp_1
		αq_2	βq_1	Rq_1	Lq_1	L	$\wedge Lp_0$	R
α	L	R	$|L$	$\wedge R$			
β	L	R	$\wedge L$	$|R$			

Fig. 25

obtained by the combination of Fig. 14 and Fig. 18. We first rewrite the states of Fig. 18 as p_0, p_1, and p_2, in order to keep them distinct from the states of Fig. 14, and we replace the symbol "!" in Fig. 14 by p_2. We then put these modified tables together, as in Fig. 25. The empty spaces represent input pairs which will never occur in the problem under consideration. (Any output triple could be put in each of these spaces.) Fig. 25 describes a process in which, first, a given pair of strings of strokes is changed into the string which represents their greatest common divisor, and then, instead of stopping at "!" (configuration *XII*, Fig. 24), the machine goes into state p_2; the operation continues and converts the result into decimal form.

It is easy to see that this method may be extended to the composition of any finite number of algorithms. It follows in particular that for a numerical algorithm we can always assume that the natural numbers are given as strings of strokes, since if we can construct a matrix for that case, say $\mathfrak{A}$, then we can easily construct a matrix for doing the computation with the initial data and the result in decimal form, namely, the composition of the following three matrices: the matrix for transforming decimal representations into strokes, the matrix $\mathfrak{A}$, and the matrix for transforming strokes back into decimal form.[1]

Another method of combining algorithms is the repeated application of the same algorithm until some predetermined condition is satisfied. For instance, the algorithm for translating into decimal notation is just a repeated application of the algorithm for the transition from n to $n + 1$, which goes on until there are no more strokes left. From the functional matrix of the given algorithm and the condition for the end of the computation, we can construct a matrix for the repeated algorithm. However, the method is more complicated than that for composition, and we shall not examine it in detail.

From the examples we have analyzed, it should be clear how to construct functional matrices for other algorithms, particularly nonnumerical ones. We shall sketch the general outline for constructing the functional matrix of the word reduction algorithm of section 14. First construct matrices $\mathfrak{A}_1$, $\mathfrak{A}_2$, $\mathfrak{A}_3$, $\mathfrak{A}_4$ for performing the directed substitutions:

$$b \rightarrow acc$$
$$ca \rightarrow accc$$
$$aa \rightarrow \wedge$$
$$cccc \rightarrow \wedge$$

(For example, the machine corresponding to $\mathfrak{A}_3$ transforms any word in the alphabet $\{a, b, c\}$ into another word in which the first

---

[1] This is analogous to the operation of electronic machines which use the binary system: they must have some arrangement for translating the initial decimal data into binary form and the binary result into decimal form.

occurrence of the pair of letters *aa* is removed. If the pair *aa* does not occur, it leaves the word unchanged.) Next construct tables $\tilde{\mathfrak{A}}_1$, $\tilde{\mathfrak{A}}_2$, $\tilde{\mathfrak{A}}_3$, $\tilde{\mathfrak{A}}_4$ for repeated applications of $\mathfrak{A}_1$, $\mathfrak{A}_2$, $\mathfrak{A}_3$, $\mathfrak{A}_4$. (For example, the machine corresponding to $\tilde{\mathfrak{A}}_3$ will remove the first occurrence of *aa* from the initial word, then remove the first occurrence of *aa* from the new word, and so on, until it produces a word which has no occurrences of *aa*). Finally, the desired reduction algorithm is the composition of the matrices $\tilde{\mathfrak{A}}_1$, $\tilde{\mathfrak{A}}_2$, $\tilde{\mathfrak{A}}_3$, $\tilde{\mathfrak{A}}_4$.

10. The Basic Hypothesis of the Theory of Algorithms

35. THE BASIC HYPOTHESIS

The examples of the last chapter leave the impression that the operation of a Turing machine is like a slow-motion film of the computation required by an algorithm. We would like to know whether functional matrices can be found for other known algorithms given in various ways, for example, as verbal instructions or algebraic formulas. At this stage of our discussion it appears likely that they can. Is this really the case? How general is the concept of Turing machine and Turing functional matrix? Can we say that all algorithms can be represented as functional matrices?

The modern theory of algorithms answers these questions with the following hypothesis.

The basic hypothesis of the theory of algorithms: *All algorithms can be given in the form of functional matrices and executed by the corresponding Turing machines.*

Two questions arise:

1. What is the significance of the hypothesis for the theory of algorithms?

2. What is the basis for the hypothesis?

The basic hypothesis on the one hand speaks of "all algorithms," that is, of the general concept of algorithms, which, as we have emphasized more than once, is not a precise mathematical concept. On the other hand, it speaks of the Turing functional matrix, which is a precise mathematical concept. Its significance is that it clarifies the general but vague concept of "all algorithms" in terms of the more special but completely precise concept of Turing functional matrix. Thus, the theory of algorithms declares the object of its investigations to be all possible Turing functional matrices (Turing machines). It then becomes meaningful to raise such questions as the existence or nonexistence of an algorithm for solving some class of problems. We now understand this to mean the existence or nonexistence of a Turing machine (functional matrix) having the required properties.

Thus, the basic hypothesis justifies the adoption of the basic definition of the modern theory of algorithms, the use of which enables the vague concept of an algorithm to be identified with the precise concept of the functional matrix of a Turing machine.

What is the basis of this important hypothesis? We cannot prove it as we prove a mathematical theorem, since it is a statement about the general concept of algorithms, which is not precisely defined and is, therefore, not a proper object of mathematical discussion.

Our confidence in the validity of the hypothesis is based chiefly on experience. All known algorithms which have been developed over the thousands of years of the history of mathematics can be written in the form of Turing functional matrices. But the hypothesis is not just a statement about algorithms which have been found in the past. It also has the quite different nature of a prediction concerning the future; it says that whenever any instructions are given as an algorithm, no matter what their form or elementary operations, it will be possible to give them as a Turing functional matrix. In this sense the basic hypothesis may be compared to a physical law, for example, the law of the conservation of energy, where the weight of vast experience in the past is judged to be a sufficient basis for predictions of future events.

36. HISTORICAL REMARKS

In the last chapter we mentioned two ways of constructing more complicated algorithms from known algorithms: composition and iteration. We could have given a longer list. However, all of the known methods are such that as soon as the initial algorithms are given as functional matrices, the composite algorithms can also be given as functional matrices. In particular, we saw for the composition of algorithms how the given functional matrices are used to construct a new matrix. In addition, we recall the following, which was mentioned in section 26. When there arose an acute necessity for an exact notion of *algorithm*, many mathematicians undertook to find a standard form for algorithms, sufficiently precise that it would be a proper object for mathematical investigation, and at the same time sufficiently general for representing all conceivable algorithms. Besides the Turing functional matrices, several other methods were proposed. For example, A. A. Markov arrived at the *normal algorithm* (which was briefly illustrated in this book by the reduction algorithm of section 14), and Gödel and Kleene arrived at the concept of *recursive algorithm* (*recursive function*). It turned out that all of these are equivalent. This cannot be considered a coincidence; it is an additional argument for the basic hypothesis.

Within the theory of algorithms itself, the basic hypothesis is not used. That is, in proving theorems in the theory, no reference is made to the basic hypothesis. Thus, a person who did not know of, or did not accept, the hypothesis would have no formal difficulties in the theory. However, he would consider what we have called the *theory of algorithms* as merely the theory of Turing functional matrices, that is, as the *theory of a particular type of algorithm*.

The author personally believes in the validity of the basic hypothesis and in the consequent estimate of the modern theory of algorithms as a *general* theory rather than simply a theory of an arbitrarily selected class of algorithms, namely the "Turing algorithms."

11. The Universal Turing Machine

Up to now we have held the point of view that different algorithms are performed by different Turing machines, each with its own functional matrix. We can, however, construct a *universal* Turing machine, capable of executing *any* algorithm, that is, in a certain sense, capable of doing the work of any Turing machine.

37. THE IMITATION ALGORITHM

In order to understand better how this is done, imagine the following situation: the tape of a machine initially contains some information $\mathfrak{A}$, and we wish to show someone how the machine processes these data. If this person is familiar with the operation of Turing machines, then it suffices to give him the initial information $\mathfrak{A}$ and the functional matrix of the machine. By writing out the configurations, as we did for the Euclidean algorithm, he can reconstruct the computation for himself. But this means that he can do the work of any Turing machine if he is given its functional matrix. The very process of imitating a machine from its functional matrix can itself be given as an exact sequence of instructions, naturally called an *imitation algorithm*, which can be carried out by someone who knows nothing about Turing machines. If he has the functional matrix of any machine and any initial configuration of the tape, he will be able to imitate the operation of the machine exactly and obtain the same result. A detailed imitation algorithm is given in the following list of instructions:

Instruction 1. Scan the (unique) cell on the tape which has a symbol underneath it.

Instruction 2. Find the column in the functional matrix headed by the symbol which appears *under* the scanned cell.

Instruction 3. Find the row headed by the symbol which appears *in* the scanned cell and note the triple of symbols which appears at the intersection of this row and column.

Instruction 4. Replace the letter in the scanned cell by the first symbol of the triple.

Instruction 5. If the second symbol of the triple is !, stop.

Instruction 6. If the second symbol of the triple is *S*, replace the symbol under the scanned cell by the third symbol of the triple.

Instruction 7. If the second symbol of the triple is *L*, erase the symbol under the scanned cell and write the third symbol of the triple under the next cell to the left.

Instruction 8. If the second symbol of the triple is *R*, erase the letter under the scanned cell and write the third symbol of the triple under the next cell to the right.

Instruction 9. Proceed to instruction 1.

38. THE UNIVERSAL TURING MACHINE

In place of our hypothetical human calculator, we can use a Turing machine; this will be a *universal* machine, capable of doing the work of any other Turing machine. In other words, the imitation algorithm, written above as nine verbal instructions, can also be given as a Turing functional matrix (the universal matrix). The complete proof of this fact, which is itself one more confirmation of the basic hypothesis, is too cumbersome to be included here. We shall limit ourselves to some general remarks concerning the form of the universal machine.

The initial information of the imitation algorithm includes the functional matrix and the initial configuration of the imitated machine. The algorithm transforms the initial configuration into a final configuration, representing the result which would be obtained by the imitated machine. A universal machine must do the same. We have the following two difficulties to overcome.

1. We cannot put the functional matrix and initial configuration of the imitated machine directly on the tape of the universal machine, for here, as in all Turing machines, all information is arranged one-dimensionally (that is, in a single row) on the tape. But the functional matrices we have given have been "two-dimensional," with several rows; the same is true of the configurations, in which the state-symbols appear below the tape.

2. The universal machine (like all Turing machines) uses a fixed finite external alphabet. With this alphabet we must be able to represent all possible matrices and configurations, which may in turn use alphabets with any number of letters.

Therefore, we must first devise some method of writing functional matrices and configurations which meets the requirements of Turing machines, namely, the one-dimensionality of the information and the finiteness of the alphabet. Instead of a two-dimensional functional matrix, with k rows and m columns, we write a sequence of mk consecutive quintuples of symbols, where the first symbol of a quintuple corresponds to the label of the row of the matrix, the second to the label of the column, and the last three make up the triple which appears at the intersection of the column and row in question.

For example, instead of the table of Fig. 12, we write

$$\wedge q_1 \wedge R q_4 \wedge q_2 \wedge L q_3 \ldots \qquad (\Omega)$$

The original table can obviously be recovered from this line in a unique manner. Similarly, we represent a configuration by writing the state-symbol to the right of the scanned cell, rather than under it. Thus configuration IV of Fig. 24 would be written

$$| | | | | q_4 | .$$

39. CODED GROUPS OF SYMBOLS

To characterize a given functional matrix and configuration, it makes no difference which letters we use in the external and internal alphabets. For instance, if we were to replace the letter β in the table of Fig. 12 by the letter b, this would in no way affect our discussion of the machine. It is important only that different objects be represented by different symbols, and that we be able to distinguish the state-symbols and tape-motion symbols from the external alphabet.

Taking these things into account, we shall replace each letter in a row Ω by a series of zeros and ones (a *coded group*), such that each appearance of a given letter is replaced by the same coded group. As a result, Ω will be changed into some row Ω' of 0's and 1's. In order that Ω may be recovered from Ω', the method of coding must satisfy the following conditions.

(1) Ω' can be broken into its various coded groups in exactly one way.

(2) There must be a rule (an algorithm) for distinguishing between the coded groups for the shifts (L, R, and S), the state-symbols, and the symbols of the external alphabet.

These two conditions are met by the following method of coding.

1. For the coded groups we take $3 + k + m$ words of the form

$$100\ldots01$$

(a string of 0's between two 1's).

A row Ω' can then be broken into its coded groups simply by cutting between consecutive 1's.

2. The code is as follows:

Symbol	Coded Group
L	101
S	1001
R	10001

		Coded Group	
external alphabet	$\begin{cases} s_1 \\ s_2 \\ \ldots \\ s_k \end{cases}$	$\begin{aligned} &100001 \text{ 4 zeros} \\ &10000001 \text{ 6 zeros} \\ &\ldots\ldots\ldots\ldots \\ &100\ldots001\ 2(k+1) \\ &\text{zeros} \end{aligned}$	$\left.\begin{aligned} &\text{an even} \\ &\text{number} \\ &\text{of zeros,} \\ &\text{greater} \\ &\text{than 2} \end{aligned}\right.$
state-symbols	$\begin{cases} q_1 \\ q_2 \\ \ldots \\ q_m \end{cases}$	$\begin{aligned} &1000001 \text{ 5 zeros} \\ &100000001 \text{ 7 zeros} \\ &\ldots\ldots\ldots\ldots \\ &100\ldots001\ 2(m+1)+1 \\ &\text{zeros} \end{aligned}$	$\left.\begin{aligned} &\text{an odd} \\ &\text{number} \\ &\text{of zeros,} \\ &\text{greater} \\ &\text{than 3} \end{aligned}\right.$

In this code with $s_1 = \wedge$, Ω' will be

100001100000110000110001100000000000110001100000001100011011 0000000001....

Such rows of 0's and 1's, coded from functional matrices or configurations, will be called *coded functional matrices* or *coded configurations*, respectively. In this code, a given functional matrix or configuration can easily be recovered in its original form. (Instead of 0 and 1, we could of course have used any other two symbols, for instance, a and b).

40. ALGORITHM FOR THE UNIVERSAL TURING MACHINE

We can now transform instructions 1–9 for the imitation algorithm from their verbal form into an algorithm which will transform the coded functional matrix and the coded initial configuration into the coded final configuration. Here are a few examples:

Instruction 1. In the coded configuration scan that coded group which appears directly to the left of the (unique) coded group with an odd number (>3) of zeros.

Instructions 2 and 3. In the coded matrix find the adjacent pair of groups which are identical with the pair of groups mentioned in instruction 1.

Instruction 6. If the second part of the triple of coded groups being examined is the group 1001, then in the coded configuration replace the coded group having an odd number (>3) of zeros by the third group of the triple.

By further analysis of this algorithm, we can reduce any operation performed on a coded group to a chain of the standard operations of Turing machines (changing one symbol into another, shifting one space to the right or left, etc.). One should note that other letters besides 0 and 1 will have to appear in the exterior alphabet of the universal machine, for example, a letter to separate the coded functional matrix from the coded configuration and letters to play the role of temporary "reminders" during the examination of the 0's and 1's (see the program for the Euclidean algorithm in section 33).

In consequence of this analysis, the imitation algorithm is expressible as the functional matrix of a Turing machine. This is then the matrix of the universal machine. If a machine A will solve some problem, then so will the universal machine, if it is given the coded initial configuration and the coded functional matrix of A.

Given the existence of the universal machine, any functional matrix (or coded functional matrix) may be viewed in two ways.

1. The functional matrix describes the logical unit of a special Turing machine for solving the corresponding problem. (This is the point of view which we adopted originally.)

2. The table describes a *program* to be used by the universal machine to solve the corresponding problem.

We note in conclusion that modern electronic machines are like the universal machine, in that, in addition to the initial data for a given problem, we also put the program for solving it into the memory. Electronic machines are also characterized by a division of the memory into an internal and an external part, where the external memory may be, say, a magnetic tape or drum. But the external memory of a Turing machine is infinite, whereas the external memory of any real machine is, of course, finite.

This essential difference between real machines and the Turing machine is, of course, unavoidable. At the same time, it is important to realize that the external memory of any real machine can be increased arbitrarily without changing the construction of the machine, for example, by just splicing on additional tape.

12. Algorithmically Unsolvable Problems

41. CHURCH'S THEOREM

Having passed from the vague concept of algorithm to the precise concept of Turing machine, we can now make precise the important question of whether a given class of problems can be solved by an algorithm. We now understand this question to mean the following: Does there exist a Turing machine for solving the given class of problems? (See Chapter 8 for the meaning of "A Turing machine solves a given class of problems.")

There are problems for which the theory of algorithms gives the answer "no." One of the first of these was discovered by the American mathematician A. Church in 1936 (see A. Church, "An Unsolvable Problem of Elementary Number Theory" in *American Journal of Mathematics*, Vol. 58). This problem is concerned with deducibility (see section 25).

CHURCH'S THEOREM. *The deducibility problem cannot be solved algorithmically.*

This not only explains the failure of all previous attempts to construct the corresponding algorithm, but shows such attempts to have been inherently futile.

42. THE SELFCOMPUTABILITY PROBLEM

Proofs of impossibility in the theory of algorithms are characterized by the same mathematical rigor as proofs of impossibility in other branches of mathematics (for example, the proof of the impossibility of trisecting an angle with compass and straightedge or of finding a common measure for a side of a square and its diagonal). We shall sketch such a proof for the *selfcomputability problem.*

Consider any configuration in a Turing machine. Two cases are possible:

1. The machine is applicable to this configuration; that is, starting from this configuration, the machine will arrive at a stop order after a finite number of steps.

2. The machine is applicable to this configuration; that is, it never reaches a stop order no matter how long it runs.

The following general problem arises.

Applicability problem. Given the functional matrix of any machine and some configuration for it, determine whether the machine is applicable to the configuration. This is a typical problem in the construction of algorithms, since to solve it one has to find a general method (an *algorithm* or a *machine*) which for *any* machine and *any* configuration gives the answer to the question of whether the machine is applicable to the configuration.

Suppose now that on the tape of a Turing machine there appears the machine's own coded functional matrix, written in the alphabet of the machine. If the machine is applicable to this configuration, we shall call it *selfapplicable;* otherwise we shall call it *nonselfapplicable.* This leads us to the following less general problem:

Selfcomputability problem. Given any coded functional matrix, determine whether the corresponding machine is selfapplicable or nonselfapplicable.

THEOREM. *The selfcomputability problem is algorithmically unsolvable.* This theorem obviously implies the algorithmic unsolvability of the applicability problem.

Proof. Assume to the contrary that there exists a machine *A* which solves the selfcomputability problem. *A* will transform every selfcomputable functional matrix into some symbol σ (denoting selfcomputability) and every nonselfcomputable functional matrix into a different symbol τ (denoting nonselfcomputability). From *A* we can construct another machine *B* with the following properties. As before, it transforms all nonselfcomputable matrices into τ, but it is inapplicable to selfcomputable matrices. Such a machine can be constructed by modifying the functional matrix of *A* so that when the symbol σ appears, instead of stopping, the machine repeatedly scans the symbol σ without erasure.

Thus, *B* is applicable to all nonselfcomputable matrices and inapplicable to all selfcomputable matrices. But this leads to a contradiction:

1. Suppose that the machine *B* is selfcomputable. Then it is applicable to its own coded functional matrix *B'*. But since *B* is applicable only to the coded functional matrices of nonselfcomputable machines, this means that *B* is nonselfcomputable.

2. Suppose that B is nonselfcomputable. Then it is inapplicable to B', which means that B must be selfcomputable. This contradiction proves the theorem.

One can establish various cases of algorithmic unsolvability and various other general problems arising in the theory of Turing machines on the basis of the above theorem.

43. COVERING PROBLEMS; THE TRANSLATABILITY PROBLEM

One widely used proof method consists of the following. Suppose that to each problem a_i of a class of problems $\{a_i\}$, one can associate a problem $f(a_i)$ of some class $\{b_i\}$ in such a way that from a solution to the problem $f(a_i)$ one can derive a solution to the problem a_i. It is natural in this case to say that the problem class $\{b_i\}$ *covers* the problem class $\{a_i\}$. Under these conditions it is also clear that if there is an algorithm for solving the class of problems $\{b_i\}$, it can be translated into an algorithm for solving the class of problems $\{a_i\}$. If, however, it has been established that the class of problems $\{a_i\}$ is algorithmically unsolvable, it follows that the class $\{b_i\}$ is likewise algorithmically unsolvable. Such a situation is often used to establish algorithmic unsolvability. Specifically, for a given problem $\mathfrak{B}$ a problem u is found such that $\mathfrak{B}$ covers u but u is algorithmically unsolvable. Let us give an example of an unsolvability proof using this method.

The translatability problem. For any given Turing machine M and any two configurations for it, K_1 and K_2, if K_1 is taken as the initial configuration for M, does the configuration K_2 ever turn up during the processing, either as the final configuration or as some intermediate configuration?

From the Turing machine M we can construct a new Turing machine M^* with the following property.

Let K be any configuration for M.

1. If M is nonapplicable to K, then M^* is nonapplicable to K.

2. If M is applicable to K, then M^* is applicable to K, and the final configuration consists of τ in the scanned cell and blanks in all the other cells, where τ is any symbol not in the external alphabet for M.

For any machine M, let P_M be the applicability problem for M, and let $f(P_M)$ be the translatability problem for M^*. If $f(P_M)$ is solvable, then there is a machine which determines for every configuration K whether or not M^* transforms it into K^*; but M^* transforms K into K^* if and only if M is applicable to K (see the construction of M^*), which means that the machine which solves $f(P_M)$ also solves P_M. Thus, the translatability problem, since it contains $\{f(P_M)\}$, covers $\{P_M\}$, the applicability problem. It follows from this and the algorithmic unsolvability of the applicability problem that the translatability problem is also algorithmically unsolvable.

Furthermore, the translatability problem remains algorithmically unsolvable if K_2 is restricted to final configurations.

44. HISTORICAL REMARKS

Algorithmic unsolvability was first established for problems in mathematical logic (the deducibility problem) and in the theory of algorithms (for example, the selfcomputability problem). There later turned out to be similar, but less general, problems in many other branches of mathematics. Among the most important are a series of algebraic problems which reduce to different variants of the word problem.

The word problem for associative calculi was formulated as early as 1914 by the Norwegian mathematician Thue; he gave algorithms in some associative calculi of a special type. Since then there have been many efforts to construct a general algorithm which could be used for any associative calculus and any pair of words in it. In 1946 and 1947, the Soviet mathematician A. A. Markov and the American mathematician Emil Post independently constructed examples of associative calculi for which the word problem cannot be solved algorithmically. Thus, there is *a fortiori* no algorithm for determining word equivalence in arbitrary calculi. Then on the basis of this result A. A. Markov and his students established the impossibility of finding algorithms for a wide class of associative calculi.

In the next section we shall give one of the proofs of the theorem that there is no algorithm for determining word equivalence in an arbitrary associative calculus.

In 1955 P. S. Novikov created a great stir in the mathematical world by demonstrating the algorithmic unsolvability of the identity problem in group theory. This problem amounts to the word equivalence problem for a special class of calculi, namely those in which for every letter a of the alphabet, there is a letter α of the alphabet (possibly equal to a) such that

$$a\alpha \longrightarrow \wedge$$

appears in the list of admissible substitutions. The significance of this condition becomes clear if, as in section 14, we interpret a letter as an elementary transformation and a word as the *product* of the elementary transformations corresponding to the letters in the word. In this case, the empty letter corresponds to the identity transformation (the transformation which leaves all elements where they are). The existence of the admissible substitutions $a\alpha - \wedge$ then means that for every elementary transformation a there exists an elementary transformation α such that the application of a followed by α is the identity transformation. Without going into further detail, it should be noted that the investigation of such sets of transformations, called *groups of transformations,* is of considerable practical and theoretical interest, the concept of group being one of the most important in modern mathematics.

It is well to realize that the very important results of Markov and Post referred to above still allowed no conclusions to be drawn about the identity problem in group theory. This was because the calculi constructed by Post and Markov did not satisfy the group axiom given above. Therefore, there was still hope for the construction of an algorithm for this problem, and efforts continued to be made until Novikov's result was published. Novikov constructed an example of a calculus satisfying the group axiom, for which no algorithm exists. Therefore, a general axiom for all groups is likewise impossible.

The examples constructed by Markov and Post were very complicated and involved hundreds of admissible substitutions. The problem of finding a simpler example has recently been solved by several people. For example, G. S. Tsentin constructed the calculus of the example in section 12, which contains only seven admissible substitutions, and for which the word problem cannot be solved algorithmically.

The discovery of algorithmically unsolvable problems gave rise to a situation in which a mathematician trying to construct some algorithm must consider the possibility that the algorithm does not even exist. Therefore, paralleling the efforts to construct the desired algorithm, efforts must be made to prove the nonexistence of this algorithm. Thus, the solution to such a problem can be either

         1) the discovery of the algorithm

or

         2) a proof of its nonexistence.

In section 3, we described Hilbert's problem on Diophantine equations. For half a century, fruitless efforts have been made to construct an algorithm for this problem. More recently, efforts have been made in the opposite direction, that is, to prove that there is no such algorithm. Although there is still no final result, the partial results which have been obtained so far make it seem likely that Hilbert's problem is algorithmically unsolvable.

13. The Nonexistence of an Algorithm for the General Word Problem

In this chapter it is proved that *there is no algorithm for determining word equivalence in an arbitrary calculus*. This proof is in two parts.

In the first part associative calculi π with directed substitutions $P \rightarrow Q$ are considered (see section 11). For such calculi, which may be called asymmetric calculi, we consider the problem of translatability. A word R is said to be translatable into a word S if there exists a deductive chain

$$R \longrightarrow R_1 \longrightarrow R_2 \longrightarrow \cdots \longrightarrow R_k \longrightarrow S,$$

where the arrow indicates that the preceding word can be transformed into the following one by the application of one of the directed substitutions. It is established that there is no algorithm for determining the translatability of words in an arbitrary asymmetric calculus. From the calculus π we can derive a calculus π' obtained by replacing each of the directed substitutions $P \rightarrow Q$ by the corresponding undirected substitution $P-Q$.

Obviously, if a word R is translatable into a word S in the calculus π, then these words are equivalent in π'. The converse assertion is not generally true, since in establishing equivalence, the converse $Q \rightarrow P$ of any admissible directed substitution $P \rightarrow Q$ may also be applied. Hence, the result obtained for asymmetric calculi does not automatically extend to the equivalence problem. In the second part this difficulty is overcome and the unsolvability theorem for the equivalence problem is proved.

45. NONEXISTENCE OF AN ALGORITHM FOR DETERMINING TRANSLATABILITY

THEOREM 1. *There is no algorithm which determines for every pair of words R and S in an asymmetric calculus whether R is translatable into S.*

The *proof* of Theorem 1 is accomplished by reducing the translatability problem for asymmetric calculi to the translatability problem for Turing machines. Inasmuch as the latter is algorithmically unsolvable, so is the former.

Consider any configuration for a Turing machine. We shall call the following cells of this configuration *active:*

(a) the scanned cell;

(b) the cells which contain a symbol other than the empty symbol;

(c) the cells which lie between cells of type (a) or (b).

The set of all active cells forms a continuous block on the tape, its *active* part. Some configurations are represented in Fig. 26, with

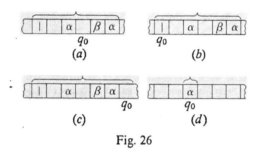

Fig. 26

their active parts marked. The scanned cell in Fig. 26a is an interior cell of the active part of the tape; that is, it is not either the leftmost or the rightmost cell of the active part. We shall call such a configuration *interior*, as opposed to configurations such as those of Fig. 26b, 26c, and 26d, which we shall call respectively *left, right,* and *unit* configurations.

Let the external alphabet of a machine be

$$s_1, s_2, \ldots, s_m$$

and its internal alphabet

$$q_1, q_2, \ldots, q_k.$$

Let us introduce one more letter h (which does not enter into either of the above alphabets) to denote the boundaries of the active portion of the tape. Every configuration can then be represented as a word hRh, where the word R is constructed as in section 38. We shall call these words C-words (configuration words).

For example, from the configurations of Fig. 26 we obtain the words

$$h| \wedge \alpha \wedge q_0\beta\alpha h; \quad h|q_0 \quad \alpha \wedge \beta\alpha h;$$
$$h| \wedge \alpha \wedge \beta\alpha \wedge q_0 h; \quad h\alpha q_0 h.$$

We now associate with the machine M a calculus π_M defined as follows.

1. The alphabet of π_M consists of the letter h and all letters of the alphabets of M. Note that while every C-word is a word in the calculus π_M, not every word in π_M is a C-word. For example, the letter q_1 appears twice in the word $hs_1q_1s_1q_1h$, which is impossible in a C-word.

2. The (directed) substitutions in π_M are constructed in such a way as to guarantee the admissibility of those transformations of C-words which correspond to the execution of instructions in the machine.

Consider an instruction of the form

$$sq \longrightarrow s'Sq', \tag{1}$$

in which the tape is not moved. It is easy to see that the same cells are active after the execution of such an instruction as before. Comparing the C-word before and after the execution of the instruction, we see that the pair of letters sq has merely been replaced by the pair of letters $s'q'$. Thus, to the instruction (1) in the Turing machine we associate the directed substitution in the calculus π_M

$$sq \longrightarrow s'q'.$$

If an instruction moves the tape, then the active part of the tape can change, depending on the type of configuration (interior, left, etc.) and the shift direction (left, right). Thus, we do not have a single substitution corresponding to the instruction (as in the case of instruction (1)), but rather a set of several substitutions.

EXAMPLE. The instruction

$$|q_0 \longrightarrow \wedge Rq_2$$

from the functional matrix for addition gives rise to the configuration transformations shown in Fig. 27.

In Fig. 27a, the same part of the tape remains active. In Fig. 27b and 27c, the active part shrinks and expands respectively. In Fig. 27d, the active part is shifted but remains the same size.

94

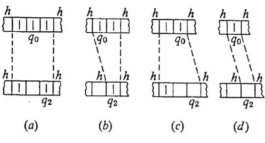

Fig. 27

For the corresponding C-words we have the transformations represented in Table 3.

TABLE 3

Initial C-word	Transformed C-word
$h \vert\vert q_0 \vert h$	$h \vert \wedge \vert q_2 h$
$h \vert q_0 \vert h$	$h \vert q_2 h$
$h \vert\vert q_0 h$	$h \vert \wedge\wedge q_2 h$
$h \vert q_0 h$	$h \wedge q_2 h$

It is easy to see that the words in the right-hand column cannot be derived from the corresponding words in the left-hand column by applying the same directed substitution.

We shall now show how to construct the system of directed substitutions corresponding to instructions of the form

$$sq \longrightarrow s'Rq'. \tag{2}$$

(The case of instructions of the form $sq \longrightarrow s'Lq'$ is treated analogously.)

We introduce the following notation: if the cell immediately to the left of the scanned cell is active, we denote its contents by σ; similarly, τ denotes the contents of the cell immediately to the right of the scanned cell, provided that it is active. Note that σ or τ or both could be the empty symbol.

We shall classify the substitutions corresponding to instruction (2) according to the type of configuration:

1. Interior configuration. The C-word contains an occurrence of a word $\sigma sq\tau$ (where σ and τ are any letters of the external alpha-

bet of the machine). With each such word we associate the substitution

$$\sigma s q \tau \longrightarrow \sigma s' \tau q'.$$

2. Left configuration. The C-word contains an occurrence of a word $h s q \tau$. We associate with it the substitution

$$hsq\tau \longrightarrow hs'\tau q' \text{ if } s' \neq \wedge,$$
$$hsq\tau \longrightarrow h\tau q' \text{ if } s' = \wedge.$$

The latter substitution reflects the fact that the cell containing s becomes inactive (see Fig. 28).

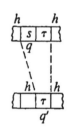

Fig. 28

3. Right configuration. The C-word contains an occurrence of a word $\sigma s q h$, with which we associate the substitution

$$\sigma s q h \longrightarrow \sigma s' \wedge q'h,$$

which reflects the fact that the active part of the tape is enlarged (see Fig. 29).

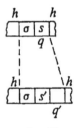

Fig. 29

4. Unit configuration. The C-word is of the form $h s q h$; with it we associate the substitution

$$hsqh \longrightarrow hs' \wedge q'h \text{ if } s' \neq \wedge,$$
$$hsqh \longrightarrow h \wedge q'h \text{ if } s' = \wedge.$$

The latter substitution reflects the fact that the active part of the tape is shifted (see Fig. 30).

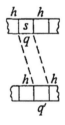

Fig. 30

This concludes the enumeration of all the directed substitutions in π_M which arise from machine instructions of the form (2).

EXAMPLE. For the Turing machine Σ for addition (see section 31), construct the corresponding calculus π_Σ.

The alphabet of π_Σ is

$$|, \wedge, *, h.$$

The instruction $\wedge q_2 \longrightarrow |S q_1$ corresponds to the substitution

$$\wedge q_2 \longrightarrow |q_1.$$

96

The instruction $|q_0 \longrightarrow \wedge Rq_2$ corresponds to the substitutions:

Interior
$$
\begin{cases}
|\,|q_0| \longrightarrow |\wedge|q_2, \\
|\,|q_0 \wedge \longrightarrow |\wedge \wedge q_2, \\
|\,|q_0^* \longrightarrow |\wedge^* q_2, \\
\wedge|q_0| \longrightarrow \wedge \wedge|q_2, \\
\wedge|q_0 \wedge \longrightarrow \wedge \wedge \wedge q_2, \\
\wedge|q_0^* \longrightarrow \wedge \wedge^* q_2, \\
{}^*|q_0| \longrightarrow {}^*\wedge|q_2, \\
{}^*|q_0 \wedge \longrightarrow {}^*\wedge \wedge q_2, \\
{}^*|q_0^* \longrightarrow {}^*\wedge^* q_2;
\end{cases}
$$

Left
$$
\begin{cases}
h|q_0| \longrightarrow h|q_2, \\
h|q_0 \wedge \longrightarrow h\wedge q_2, \\
h|q_0^* \longrightarrow h^* q_2;
\end{cases}
$$

Right
$$
\begin{cases}
|\,|q_0 h \longrightarrow |\wedge \wedge q_2 h, \\
\wedge|q_0 h \longrightarrow \wedge \wedge \wedge q_2 h, \\
{}^*|q_0 h \longrightarrow {}^*\wedge \wedge q_2 h;
\end{cases}
$$

Unit
$$
\begin{cases}
h|q_0 h \longrightarrow h\wedge q_2 h.
\end{cases}
$$

The substitutions corresponding to the other instructions can be enumerated in exactly the same way.

Now note the following properties of the calculus π_M constructed from a given machine M:

Assertion 1. Every C-word for the machine M is a word in π_M.

Assertion 2. If $\mathfrak{A}$ is the C-word corresponding to a configuration $\mathfrak{A}$, then at most one substitution in π_M is applicable to it. This substitution transforms $\mathfrak{A}$ into the C-word $\mathfrak{B}$ corresponding to the configuration $\mathfrak{B}$ into which the machine transforms $\mathfrak{A}$.

Assertion 3. If $\mathfrak{A}$ is a final configuration for the machine M, then no substitution is applicable to $\mathfrak{A}$.

It follows directly from these assertions that the question of whether a configuration $\mathfrak{A}$ is translatable into a configuration $\mathfrak{B}$ in the machine M is equivalent to the question of whether the C-word $\mathfrak{A}$ is translatable into the C-word $\mathfrak{B}$ in the calculus π_M. In other words, the translatability problem for asymmetric calculi covers the translatability problem for Turing machines. This proves Theorem 1.

If $\mathfrak{B}$ represents only the final configurations for the machine M, we obtain the following theorem.

THEOREM 2. *There is no algorithm which allows one to determine for an arbitrary asymmetric calculus and an arbitrary pair of words $\tilde{\mathfrak{A}}$ and $\tilde{\mathfrak{B}}$, of which the second is reduced, whether or not $\tilde{\mathfrak{A}}$ is translatable into $\tilde{\mathfrak{B}}$.*

46. UNSOLVABILITY OF THE WORD EQUIVALENCE PROBLEM

Let R and S be two C-words in the calculus π_M. If R is translatable into S by directed substitutions, then R is *a fortiori* equivalent to S in π_M. Do any further equivalences arise if the directed substitutions are replaced by the corresponding undirected substitutions? The answer to this question is given in the following lemma.

LEMMA. *If S is a final C-word and R is equivalent to S in π_M (admitting undirected substitutions), then R is translatable into S using only the directed substitutions of π_M.*

The algorithmic unsolvability of the word equivalence problem in associative calculi follows directly from this lemma. For if there were an algorithm for determining whether or not words are equivalent, it would solve the translatability problem in asymmetric calculi. But by Theorem 2, there is no such algorithm.

Proof of the lemma. If $R \sim S$, then there exists a deductive chain leading from R to S:

$$R = R_1 - R_2 - R_3 - \cdots - R_{k-1} - R_k = S. \tag{3}$$

Let R_j and R_{j+1} be two adjacent words in this chain. If the passage from R_j to R_{j+1} is accomplished by applying a directed substitution of the form $P \to Q$, we write $R_j \to R_{j+1}$; and if it is accomplished by applying the converse of one of the given directed substitutions (see p. 92), we write $R_j \leftarrow R_{j+1}$. Now consider the following possibilities for three consecutive words in the chain (3):

$$R_{j-1} \leftarrow R_j \to R_{j+1}, \tag{4}$$
$$R_{j-1} \to R_j \leftarrow R_{j+1}. \tag{5}$$

By virtue of assertion 2, the words R_{j-1} and R_{j+1} must coincide in case (4), since only one substitution is applicable to the word R_j. Hence, such a triple of words can be eliminated from a deductive chain simply by deleting two of its elements (say, R_{j-1} and R_j). In case (5), however, the words R_{j-1} and R_{j+1} can be different. In terms of the Turing machine this means that the configuration of the machine does not uniquely determine the preceding configuration.

Now turn to the chain (3). Inasmuch as R_k is a final configuration, we can only have $R_{k-1} \rightarrow R_k$ (see assertion 3). If all the arrows point to the right, the lemma is proved. Suppose that there are arrows pointing left, the last one being, say, from R_j to R_{j-1}. Then there is a triple

$$R_{j-1} \leftarrow R_j \rightarrow R_{j+1},$$

from which two words can be deleted, giving us a shorter deductive chain leading from R to S. Continuing this elimination process, we finally arrive at a chain which cannot be made any shorter; this will then have to contain only arrows pointing right. Thus, R is translatable into S by the admissible directed substitutions.

Concluding Remarks

In conclusion, let us make several general observations.

1. In the first place, theorems on the algorithmic unsolvability of some class of problems should not be a cause of despair. Such a theorem only proves that there is no algorithm capable of handling the *entire class* of problems. This does not mean that among the particular problems comprising the class there are none which can be solved algorithmically. For example, the theorem proved in section 42 should not be taken to mean that for a specific machine it is in principle impossible to establish whether or not it is self-computable. It only means that the class of problems is too wide; that there is no single algorithm which will solve *all* problems of the class. In such situations, one tries to construct more and more general algorithms for solving more general subclasses of problems of the given type.

2. In the second place, theorems of algorithmic unsolvability show that mathematics does not reduce to the construction of algorithms. Even in comparatively narrow areas of mathematics (for example, the theory of finitely generated groups), there are extensive problems which cannot be solved by any kind of automaton (Turing machine with a finite number of states and a finite memory). This shows the absurdity of statements about machines fully replacing the creative work of science.

3. At the same time, it must be recognized that the range of application of algorithms is very large and is not restricted to the computational processes which arise in mathematics. For many processes which are usually considered difficult and complicated, it is possible to construct algorithms which are basically rather simple; the practical difficulties connected with carrying these processes out arise from the fact that the algorithms often require an enormous number of operations to be performed (even though each operation itself is simple). This remark applies in particular to games (and especially to chess), where victory usually depends on the ability to survey a large number of possibilities in order to determine the optimal move.

With the construction of high-speed computing machines, the number of practical algorithms was enlarged considerably.

4. Finally, we mention once again that every real computing machine may be considered as only an approximate model of a Turing machine. That is, every real machine has a limited external memory, whereas the Turing machine has an infinite tape. Of course, it is physically impossible to construct an infinite memory, but a significant increase in the size of machine memories, in comparison to the level previously achieved, is not only desirable, but quite possible. Thus, increasing the size of external memories and increasing calculating speeds should bring further great advances in the development of computing automata.

Bibliography

1. Turing, A. M. "On Computable Numbers, with an Application to the Entscheidungsproblem," *Proceedings of the London Mathematical Society,* Series 2, Vol. 42 (1936–37), pp. 230–65.
2. Kleene, S. C., *Introduction to Metamathematics.* Princeton, N. J.: Van Nostrand, 1952.
3. Davis, Martin, *Computability and Unsolvability.* New York: McGraw-Hill, 1958.
4. Rózsa, Péter, *Rekursive Funktionen.* Berlin: Akademie Verlag, 1957.
5. *Advances in Computers,* Vol. 1 (Alt, Franz L., ed.). New York: Academic Press, 1960.
6. Beth, E. W., *Foundations of Mathematics.* Groningen: North-Holland Publishing Co., 1959.
7. McCracken, D. D., *Digital Computer Programming.* New York: John Wiley, 1957.

TOPICS IN MATHEMATICS